THE MORAVIANS IN GEORGIA.

AUGUST GOTTLIEB SPANGENBERG.

THE MORAVIANS IN GEORGIA

1735–1740

ADELAIDE L. FRIES
WINSTON-SALEM
N. C.

Southern Historical Press, Inc.
Greenville, South Carolina

This volume was reproduced from
an 1905 edition located in the
Publisher's private Library

All rights reserved. No part of this publication may be reproduced, stored in a retrieval system or transmitted in any form or by any means without the prior written permission of the publisher.

Please Direct All Correspondence and Book Orders to:

Southern Historical Press, Inc.
1071 Park West Blvd.
Greenville, SC   29611

Copyrighted: Adelaide L. Fries. 1905
ISBN #978-1-63914-308-5
Printed in the United States of America

PREFACE.

In the life of any individual, association, or nation, there will probably be one or more occurrences which may be considered as success or failure according to the dramatic features of the event and the ultimate results. Of this the Battle of Bunker Hill is a striking example. On the morning of June 17th, 1775, a force of British soldiers attacked a small body of raw, ill-equipped American volunteers, who had fortified a hill near Boston, and quickly drove them from their position. By whom then was the Bunker Hill Monument erected? By the victors in that first engagement of the Revolution? No, but by proud descendants of the vanquished, whose broader view showed them the incalculable benefits arising from that seeming defeat, which precipitated the great struggle, forcing every man in the Colonies to take a position squarely for or against the American Cause, convinced the timid that only proper equipment would be needed to enable the American army to hold its own against the foe, and taught the British that they were dealing, not with hot-headed rebels who would run at first sight of the dreaded "red coats," but with patriots who would stand their ground so long as a charge of powder remained, or gunstocks could be handled as clubs.

Very much the same line of argument may be applied to the first attempt of the Moravian Church to establish a settlement on the American Continent. The story is usually passed over by historians in a few short paragraphs, and yet without the colony in Georgia, the whole history of the Renewed Church of the Unitas Fratrum would have been very different. Without that movement the Moravian Church might never have been established in England, without it the great Methodist denomination might never have come into being, without it the American Moravian provinces, North or South, might not have been planned. Of course Providence might have provided other means for the accomplishment of these ends, but certain it is that in the actual development of all these things the "unsuccessful attempt" in Georgia, 1735 to 1740, played a most important part.

In preparing this history a number of private libraries, the collections of the Georgia Historical Society, the Congressional Library, the British Museum, were searched for data, but so little was found that the story, in so far as it relates to the Moravian settlement, has been drawn entirely from the original manuscripts in the Archives of the Unitas Fratrum at Herrnhut, Germany, with some additions from the Archives at Bethlehem, Pa., and Salem, N. C. For the general history of Georgia, of the Moravian Church, and of the Wesleys, Steven's History of Georgia, Hamilton's History of the Moravian Church, Levering's History of Bethlehem, Pa., Some Fathers of the American Moravian

Church, by de Schweinitz, Strobel's History of the Salzburgers, Tyreman's Oxford Methodists, and Wesley's Journal have been most largely used.

The history of the Moravian settlement in Georgia falls into that period when dates are much confused through the contemporaneous use of the old style, or Julian calendar, and the new style, or Gregorian calendar. As the latter is now current everywhere, except in Russia and the Orient, it is here employed throughout, old style dates being translated where they occur in the records.

Special thanks are due to Rev. A. Glitsch, Archivist at Herrnhut, for courtesies extended while the author was examining the invaluable collection of papers entrusted to his care, and also for his supervision of the copying of such documents as were selected; to Mr. Isaac Beckett, of Savannah, for information respecting the Moravian lands; to Mr. John Jordan, of Philadelphia, for copies of deeds and other papers relating to the settlement; to Mr. W. S. Pfohl, of Salem, for assistance with the illustrations; and to Mr. John W. Fries for suggestion and inspiration for the work, and the constant encouragement and sympathetic interest without which the author's courage would have failed during the tedious years of gathering material for the book, which is now presented to those who may find in it something of explanation, something of interest, concerning the Moravian settlement in Georgia, and the broader history which the story touches on every side.

ADELAIDE L. FRIES.

AUGUST, 1904.

TABLE OF CONTENTS.

CHAPTER I. ANTECEDENT EVENTS.   PAGE.

   The Province of Georgia............................ 13
   The Salzburgers...................................... 18
   Unitas Fratum... 21
   Halle Opposition...................................... 25

CHAPTER II. NEGOTIATIONS WITH THE TRUSTEES OF GEORGIA.

   The Schwenkfelders 28
   Preliminary Steps..................................... 36
   The "First Company" 47

CHAPTER III. THE FIRST YEAR IN GEORGIA.

   The Voyage... 57
   Making a Start.. 65
   Aim and Attainment................................ 70

CHAPTER IV. REINFORCEMENTS.

   The "Second Company"........................... 89
   Four Journals.. 98
   Organization.. 122

CHAPTER V. THE SECOND YEAR IN GEORGIA.

   The English Clergymen............................ 143
   Work Among the Indians........................ 147
   The "Society".. 155
   Rumors of War....................................... 161

CHAPTER VI. DISINTEGRATION.

    Spangenberg's Visit.................................... 169
    A Closing Door.. 181
    Wesley, Ingram and Töltschig 190
    The Negro Mission 201

CHAPTER VII. CONCLUSION.

    Later Attempts in Georgia............................ 221
    The Savannah Lands.................................... 229
    Arrivals, Departures, Deaths........................ 236
    Summary 242

ILLUSTRATIONS.

August Gottlieb Spangenberg...............		Frontispiece
View of Savannah........................opposite page		18
Nicholas Lewis, Count Zinzendorf....	"	" 22
Ecce Homo........	"	" 26
Gen. James Oglethorpe...................	"	" 50
Plan of Savannah	"	" 67
Province of Georgia...........	"	" 75
Gen. James Oglethorpe...........	"	" 111
David Nitschmann, Episc...............	"	" 132
Tomochichi........	"	" 148
Count Zinzendorf, portrait bust........	"	" 160
Peter Böhler.............	"	" 190
Zeisberger Preaching to the Indians..	"	" 218
Savannah and Environs..................	"	" 229
James Habersham......................	"	" 231

THE MORAVIANS IN GEORGIA,
1735-1740.

Chapter I.
ANTECEDENT EVENTS.

THE PROVINCE OF GEORGIA.

It was in the year 1728 that the English Parliament was persuaded by James Oglethorpe, Esq.—soldier, statesman and philanthropist,—to appoint a committee to investigate the condition of the debtors confined in the Fleet and Marchalsea prisons. The lot of these debtors was a most pitiable one, for a creditor had power to imprison a man for an indefinite term of years, and the unfortunate debtor, held within the four walls of his prison, could earn no money to pay the debt that was owing, and unless friends came to his rescue, was utterly at the mercy of the oft-times barbarous jailor. The Committee, consisting of ninety-six prominent men, with Oglethorpe as Chairman, recommended and secured the redress of many grievances, and the passing of better laws for the future, but Oglethorpe and a few associates conceived a plan which they thought would eradicate the evil by striking at its very root, the difficulty which many found in earning a living in the overcrowded cities.

In 1663 King Charles II. had granted to eight

"Lords Proprietors" the portion of North America lying between the 31st and 36th degrees of latitude, enlarging the boundaries in 1665 to 29° and 36° 30'. By 1728 most of these Lords Proprietors had tired of their attempt to govern the colonies they had established in "Carolina," and in 1729 seven of the eight sold their interest to the English crown, the district being divided into "North Carolina," "South Carolina," and a more southerly portion, nominally included in the latter, which was held in reserve.

To this unused land the thoughts of Oglethorpe turned, and he and his friends addressed a memorival to the Privy Council, stating "that the cities of London, Westminster, and parts adjacent, do abound with great numbers of indigent persons, who are reduced to such necessity as to become burthensome to the public, and who would be willing to seek a livelihood in any of his majesty's plantations in America, if they were provided with a passage, and means of settling there." They therefore asked for a grant of land lying south of the Savannah River, where they wished to establish a colony in which these unfortunate men might begin life anew, and where Protestants, persecuted in some parts of Europe, might find a refuge. They also offered to take entire charge of the affair, and their petition, after passing through the usual channels, was approved by the King, George II, a charter was prepared, and the great seal was affixed June 9th, 1732.

This instrument constituted twenty-one noblemen and gentlemen a body corporate, by the name and style of "The Trustees for establishing the Colony of Georgia in America," and in them was vested full authority for the collecting of subscriptions and the expending of moneys gathered, the selection of colonists, and the making and administering of laws in Georgia; but no member of the corporation was allowed to receive a salary, or any fees, or to hold land in the new province. The undertaking was to be strictly for the good of others, not for their own pecuniary benefit. The charter granted to them "all those lands, countries, and territories situate, lying and being in that part of South Carolina, in America" between the Savannah and Altamaha, gave them permission to take over any British subjects, or foreigners willing to become such, and guaranteed to each settler the rights of an English subject, and full liberty of conscience,—Papists alone excepted. This apparently pointed exception was natural enough, since from a political standpoint the new colony was regarded as a valuable guard for the Protestant English Colonies on the north, against the Indians and Roman Catholic colonists to the south, who had been keeping the border settlers in a continual state of uneasiness, even in times of nominal peace. Moreover England had not forgotten the terrible experience of the latter half of the preceding century, when it was war to the death between Catholic and Protestant, and the latter party being the stronger the former was subjected to great and unpardonable persecution, many were executed, and all holding that faith were laid under political disabilities which lasted for a hundred and fifty years.

The plans of the Trustees were very broad. They intended "to relieve such unfortunate persons as cannot subsist here, and establish them in an orderly manner, so as to form a well regulated town. As far as their fund goes they will defray the charge of their passage to Georgia—give them necessaries, cattle, land, and subsistence, till such time as they can build their houses and clear some of their land." In this manner "many families who would otherwise starve will be provided for, and made masters of houses and lands; * * * and by giving refuge to the distressed Salzburgers and other Protestants, the power of Britain, as a reward for its hospitality, will be increased by the addition of so many religious and industrious subjects."

Each of the emigrants was to receive about fifty acres of land, including a town lot, a garden of five acres, and a forty-five acre farm, and the Trustees offered to give a tract of five hundred acres to any well-to-do man who would go over at his own expense, taking with him at least ten servants, and promising his military service in case of need.

But there was a commercial as well as a benevolent side to the designs of the Trustees, for they thought Georgia could be made to furnish silk, wine, oil and drugs in large quantities, the importing of which would keep thousands of pounds sterling in English hands which had hitherto gone to China, Persia and the Madeiras. Special provision was therefore made to secure the planting of mulberry trees as the first step towards silk culture, the other branches to be introduced as speedily as might be.

Filled with enthusiasm for their plan, the Trustees proceeded to spread abroad the most glowing descriptions of the country where the new colony was to be settled.

"The kind spring, which but salutes us here,
  Inhabits there, and courts them all the year.
Ripe fruits and blossoms on the same trees live—
  At once they promise, when at once they give.
So sweet the air, so moderate the clime,
  None sickly lives, or dies before his time.
Heaven, sure, has kept this spot of earth uncurst,
  To shew how all things were created first."

So wrote Oglethorpe, quoting the lines as the best pen picture he could give of the new land, and truly, if the colonists found the reality less roseate than they anticipated, it was not the fault of their generous, energetic leader, who spared neither pains nor means in his effort to make all things work out as his imagination had painted them.

The Trustees having, with great care, selected thirty-five families from the number who wished to go, the first emigrant ship sailed for Georgia in November, 1732, bearing about one hundred and twenty-five "sober, industrious and moral persons," and all needful stores for the establishment of the colony. Early in the following year they reached America, and Oglethorpe, having chosen a high bluff on the southern bank of the Savannah River, concluded a satisfactory treaty with Tomochichi, the chief of the nearest Indian tribe, which was later ratified in a full Council of the chiefs of all the

Lower Creeks. His fairness and courteous treatment won the hearts of all, especially of Tomochichi and his people, who for many years remained on the best of terms with the town which was now laid out upon the bluff.

THE SALZBURGERS.

The Salzburgers, referred to by name in the proposals of the Georgia Trustees, were, at this time, very much upon the mind and heart of Protestant Europe. They were Germans, belonging to the Archbishopric of Salzburg, then the most eastern district of Bavaria, but now a province of Austria. "Their ancestors, the Vallenges of Piedmont, had been compelled by the barbarities of the Dukes of Savoy to find a shelter from the storms of persecution in the Alpine passes and vales of Salzburg and the Tyrol, before the Reformation; and frequently since, they had been hunted out by the hirelings and soldiery of the Church of Rome, and condemned for their faith to tortures of the most cruel and revolting kind. In 1684-6, they were again threatened with an exterminating persecution; but were saved in part by the intervention of the Protestant States of Saxony and Brandenburg, though more than a thousand emigrated on account of the dangers to which they were exposed.

"But the quietness which they then enjoyed for nearly half a century was rudely broken in upon by Leopold, Count of Firmian and Archbishop of Salzburg, who determined to reduce them to the Papal faith and power. He began in the year 1729, and ere he ended in 1732 not far from thirty thousand

SAVANNAH, 1734.
From Engraving in the British Museum.

had been driven from their homes, to seek among the Protestant States of Europe that charity and peace which were denied them in the glens and fastnesses of their native Alps.

"The march of these Salzburgers constitutes an epoch in the history of Germany. * * * Arriving at Augsburg, the magistrates closed the gates against them, refusing them entrance to that city which, two hundred years before, through Luther and Melancthon and in the presence of Charles V and the assembled Princes of Germany, had given birth to the celebrated Augsburg Confession, for clinging to which the Salzburgers were now driven from their homes; but overawed by the Protestants, the officers reluctantly admitted the emigrants, who were kindly entertained by the Lutherans.

"The sympathies of Reformed Christendom were awakened on their behalf, and the most hospitable entertainment and assistance were everywhere given them." Only a few months after the signing of the Georgia Colony Charter, the "Society for the Propagation of Christian Knowledge" requested the Trustees to include the Salzburgers in their plans. The Trustees expressed their willingness to grant lands, and to manage any money given toward their expenses, but stated that they then held no funds which were available for that purpose.

In May, 1733, the House of Commons appropriated £10,000 to the Trustees of Georgia, "to be applied towards defraying the charges of carrying over and settling foreign and other Protestants in said colony," and over £3,000 additional having been given privately, the Trustees, at the suggestion of Herr von Pfeil, consul of Wittenberg at Regensberg, wrote to Senior Samuel Urlsperger, pastor of the Lutheran Church of St. Ann in the city of Augsburg, who had been very kind to the Salzburgers on their arrival there, "and ever afterward watched over their welfare with the solicitude of an affectionate father." On receipt of the invitation from the Trustees, seventy-eight persons decided to go to Georgia, and left Augsburg on the 21st of October, reaching Rotterdam the 27th of November, where they were joined by two ministers, Rev. Mr. Bolzius, deputy superintendent of the Latin Orphan School at Halle, and Rev. Mr. Gronau, a tutor in the same, who were to accompany them to their new home. In England they were treated with marked kindness, and when they sailed, January 19, 1734, it was with the promise of free transportation to Georgia, and support there until they could reap their first harvest from the fifty acres which were to be given to each man among them.

They reached Charlestown, South Carolina, the following March, and met General Oglethorpe, the Governor of Georgia, who was intending an immediate return to Europe, but went back to help them select a suitable place for their settlement, they preferring not to live in Savannah itself. The site chosen was about twenty-five miles from Savannah, on a large stream flowing into the Savannah River, and there they laid out their town, calling it "Ebenezer," in grateful remembrance of the Divine help that had brought them thither. Baron von Reck, who had accompanied them as Commissary of the Trustees, stayed with them until they had made a good beginning, and then returned to Europe, leaving Ebenezer about the middle of May.

UNITAS FRATRUM.

But while the Salzburgers received so much sympathy and kindness in Germany on account of their distress, other exiled Protestants, whose story was no less touching, were being treated with scant courtesy and consideration.

On the 6th of July, 1415, the Bohemian Reformer, John Hus, was burned at the stake. But those who had silenced him could not unsay his message, and at last there drew together a little body of earnest men, who agreed to accept the Bible as their only standard of faith and practice, and established a strict discipline which should keep their lives in the simplicity, purity, and brotherly love of the early Apostolic Church. This was in 1457, and the movement quickly interested the thoughtful people in all classes of society, many of whom joined their ranks. The formal organization of the Unitas Fratrum (the Unity of Brethren) followed, and its preaching, theological publications, and educational work soon raised it to great influence in Bohemia, Moravia and Poland, friendly intercourse being established with Luther, Calvin, and other Reformers as they became prominent.

Then came destruction, when the religious liberty of Bohemia and Moravia was extinguished in blood, by the Church of Rome. The great Comenius went forth, a wanderer on the face of the earth, welcomed and honored in courts and universities, introducing new educational principles that revolutionized methods of teaching, but ever longing and praying for the restoration of his Church; and by his publication of its Doctrine and Rules of Discipline, and by his careful transmission of the Episcopate which had been bestowed upon him and his associate Bishops, he did contribute largely to that renewal which he was not destined to see.

In the home lands there were many who held secretly, tenaciously, desperately, to the doctrines they loved, "in hope against hope" that the great oppression would be lifted. But the passing of a hundred years brought no relief, concessions granted to others were still denied to the children of those who had been the first "protestants" against religious slavery and corruption, and in 1722 a small company of descendants of the ancient Unitas Fratrum slipped over the borders of Moravia, and went to Saxony, Nicholas Lewis, Count Zinzendorf, having given them permission to sojourn on his estates until they could find suitable homes elsewhere.

Hearing that they had reached a place of safety, other Moravians took their lives in their hands and followed, risking the imprisonment and torture which were sure to follow an unsuccessful attempt to leave a province, the Government of which would neither allow them to be happy at home nor to sacrifice everything and go away. Among these emigrants were five young men, who went in May, 1724, with the avowed intention of trying to resusciate the Unitas Fratrum. They intended to go into Poland, where the organization of the Unitas Fratrum had lasted for a considerable time after its

NICHOLAS LEWIS, COUNT ZINZENDORF.

ruin in Bohemia, but, almost by accident, they decided to first visit Christian David, who had led the first company to Herrnhut, Saxony, and while there they became convinced that God meant them to throw in their lot with these refugees, and so remained, coming to be strong leaders in the renewed Unity.

Several years, however, elapsed before the church was re-established. One hundred years of persecution had left the Moravians only traditions of the usages of the fathers, members of other sects who were in trouble came and settled among them, bringing diverse views, and things were threatening to become very much involved, when Count Zinzendorf, who had hitherto paid little attention to them, awoke to the realization of their danger, and at once set to work to help them.

It was no easy task which he undertook, for the Moravians insisted on retaining their ancient discipline, and he must needs try to please them and at the same time preserve the bond of union with the State Church,—the Lutheran,—of which, as his tenants, they were officially considered members. His tact and great personal magnetism at last healed the differences which had sprung up between the settlers, the opportune finding of Comenius' *Ratio Disciplinae* enabled them with certainty to formulate rules that agreed with those of the ancient Unitas Fratrum, and a marked outpouring of the Holy Spirit at a Communion, August 13th, 1727, sealed the renewal of the Church.

"They walked with God in peace and love,
  But failed with one another;
While sternly for the faith they strove,
  Brother fell out with brother;
But He in Whom they put their trust,
  Who knew their frames, that they were dust,
Pitied and healed their weakness.

"He found them in His House of prayer,
  With one accord assembled,
And so revealed His presence there,
  They wept for joy and trembled;
One cup they drank, one bread they brake,
  One baptism shared, one language spake,
Forgiving and forgiven.

"Then forth they went with tongues of flame
  In one blest theme delighting,
The love of Jesus and His Name
  God's children all uniting!
That love our theme and watchword still;
  That law of love may we fulfill,
And love as we are loved."

(Montgomery.)

At this time there was no thought of separating from the State Church and establishing a distinct denomination, and Zinzendorf believed that the Unitas Fratrum could exist as a *society* working in, and in harmony with, the State Church of whatever nation it might enter. This idea, borrowed probably from Spener's *"ecclesiolae in ecclesia,"* clung to him, even after circumstances had forced the Unity to declare its independence and the validity of the ordination of its ministry, and many otherwise inexplicable things in the later policy of the Church may be traced to its influence.

HALLE OPPOSITION.

In 1734 Zinzendorf took orders in the Lutheran Church, but this, and all that preceded it, seemed to augment rather than quiet the antagonism which the development of Herrnhut aroused in certain quarters. This opposition was not universal. The Moravians had many warm friends and advocates at the Saxon Court, at the Universities of Jena and Tübingen, and elsewhere, but they also had active enemies who drew their inspiration prinicpally from the University of Halle.

The opposition of Halle seems to have been largely prompted by jealousy. In 1666 a revolt against the prevailing cold formalism of the Lutheran Church was begun by Philip Jacob Spener, a minister of that Church, who strongly urged the need for real personal piety on the part of each individual. His ideas were warmly received by some, and disliked by others, who stigmatized Spener and his disciples as "Pietists," but the doctrine spread, and in the course of time the University of Halle became its centre. Among those who were greatly attracted by the movement were Count Zinzendorf's parents and grandparents, and when he was born, May 26th, 1700, Spener was selected as his sponsor.

Being of a warm-hearted, devout nature, young

Zinzendorf yielded readily to the influence of his pious grandmother, to whose care he was left after his father's death and his mother's second marriage, and by her wish he entered the Paedagogium at Halle in 1710, remaining there six years. Then his uncle, fearing that he would become a religious enthusiast, sent him to the University of Wittenberg, with strict orders to apply himself to the study of law. Here he learned to recognize the good side of the Wittenberg divines, who were decried by Halle, and tried to bring the two Universities to a better understanding, but without result.

In 1719 he was sent on an extensive foreign tour, according to custom, and in the picture gallery of Düsseldorf saw an Ecce Homo with its inscription "This have I done for thee, what hast thou done for me?" which settled him forever in his determination to devote his whole life to the service of Christ.

Rather against his wishes, Count Zinzendorf then took office under the Saxon Government, but about the same time he bought from his grandmother the estate of Berthelsdorf, desiring to establish a centre of piety, resembling Halle. The coming of the Moravian and other refugees and their settlement at Herrnhut, near Berthelsdorf, was to him at first only an incident; but as their industry and the preaching of Pastor Rothe, whom he had put in charge of the Berthelsdorf Lutheran Church, began to attract attention, he went to Halle, expecting sympathy from his friends there. Instead he met with rebuke and disapproval, the leaders resenting the fact that he had not placed the work directly under their control, and apparently realizing, as he

ECCE HOMO
von Domenico Feti geb. 1589 zu Rom gest. 1624 zu Venedig.

did not, that the movement would probably lead to the establishment of a separate church.

In spite of their disapprobation, the work at Herrnhut prospered, and the more it increased the fiercer their resentment grew. That they, who had gained their name from their advocacy of the need for personal piety, should have been foremost in opposing a man whose piety was his strongest characteristic, and a people who for three hundred years, in prosperity and adversity, in danger, torture and exile, had held "Christ and Him Crucified" as their Confession of Faith, and pure and simple living for His sake as their object in life, is one of the ironies of history.

Nor did the Halle party confine itself to criticism. Some years later Zinzendorf was for a time driven into exile, and narrowly escaped the confiscation of all his property, while its methods of obstructing the missionary and colonizing efforts of the Moravians will appear in the further history of the Georgia colony.

Chapter II.

NEGOTIATIONS WITH THE TRUSTEES OF GEORGIA.

THE SCHWENKFELDERS.

Among those who came to share the hospitalities of Count Zinzendorf during the years immediately preceding the renewal of the Unitas Fratrum, were a company of Schwenkfelders. Their sojourn on his estate was comparatively brief, and their association with the Moravian Church only temporary, but they are of interest because their necessities led directly to the Moravian settlements in Georgia and Pennsylvania.

The Schwenkfelders took their name from Casper Schwenkfeld, a Silesian nobleman contemporary with Luther, who had in the main embraced the Reformer's doctrines, but formed some opinions of his own in regard to the Lord's Supper, and one or two other points. His followers were persecuted in turn by Lutherans and Jesuits, and in 1725 a number of them threw themselves on the mercy of Count Zinzendorf. He permitted them to stay for a while at Herrnhut, where their views served to increase the confusion which prevailed prior to the revival of 1727, about which time he moved them to Ober-Berthelsdorf.

In 1732, Zinzendorf's personal enemies accused him, before the Saxon Court, of being a dangerous man, and the Austrian Government complained that he was enticing its subjects to remove to his estates. The Count asked for a judicial investigation, which was granted, the Prefect of Görlitz spending three days in a rigid examination of the affairs of Herrnhut. The result was a most favorable report, showing the orthodoxy of the settlers, and that instead of urging emigration from Bohemia and Moravia, Zinzendorf had protested against it, receiving only those who were true exiles for conscience' sake. In spite of this the Saxon Government, a few months later, forbade him to receive any more refugees.

In April, 1733, a decree went forth that all Schwenkfelders were to leave the Kingdom of Saxony. This, of course, affected those who were living at Ober-Berthelsdorf, and a committee of four waited on Count Zinzendorf, and requested him to secure a new home for them in the land of Georgia in North America. Probably Zinzendorf, whose attention had been caught by the attractive advertisements of the Trustees, had unofficially suggested the idea to them.

Lest his opening negotiations with the English Company should foment the trouble at home, he sent his first communication to them anonymously, about the end of 1733.

"A nobleman, of the Protestant religion, connected with the most influential families of Germany, has decided to live for a time in America, without, however, renouncing his estates in Germany. But as circumstances render it inadvisable for him to take such a step hastily, he wishes to send in advance a number of families of his dependents, composed of honest, sturdy, industrious, skillful, economical people, well ordered in their domestic affairs, who, having no debts, will try to sell such possessions as they cannot take with them in order to raise the funds for establishing themselves in their new home.

"This nobleman, on his part, promises:

(1) To be governed by the King, and the English Nation, in all things, matters of conscience alone excepted; that is, he will be true to the Prince, the Protestant Succession, and Parliament in everything relating to the estates he may receive in this country, and thereto will pledge his life, and the property he may in future hold under the protection of His Majesty of Great Britain.

(2) To be surety for the dependents that he sends over, and to assume only such jurisdiction over them as is customary among English Lords on their estates.

(3) To carefully repay the English Nation such sums as may be advanced for his establishment in Georgia, and moreover, as soon as the property is in good condition, to consider it only as rented until the obligation is discharged.

(4) To assist the King and Nation, with all zeal and by all means in his power, to carry out His Majesty's designs for Georgia. He will bring to that all the insight and knowledge of a man of affairs, who from youth up has studied the most wholesome principles and laws for a State, and has had personal experience in putting them into execution; but, on the other hand, he has learned such

self-control that he will meddle with nothing in which his services are not desired.

"In consideration of these things the nobleman asks that—

(1) If more knowledge of his standing is desired he shall be expected to give it to no one except a Committee of Parliament, composed of members of both houses, appointed by his Britannic Majesty, or to a Committee of the *Collegii directoriatis* of America, who shall be empowered to grant his requests; this in view of the fact that the petitioner is a German Nobleman, whose family is well known, his father having been Ambassador to England, and his kindred among the foremost statesmen of Europe.

(2) After the Committee has received sufficient and satisfactory information it shall be silent in regard to the circumstances and his personality, as he has weighty reasons for not wishing to subject himself to criticism.

(3) He shall be given a written agreement, guaranteeing the following things:

a. That he shall receive enough land for a household of fifty to sixty persons, and for about a hundred other dependents, most of whom have a trade or profession, and all able to help build up the country.

b. That his dependents shall be given free transportation, and supplies for the voyage.

c. That they shall be taken directly to the place mentioned in the agreement.

d. That he and his agent shall have certain sums advanced to him for the expenses of the removal to Georgia, the money to be given them only when they are ready to embark in England,—payment to be made several years later, a rate of interest having been mutually agreed on, and the estate in Georgia being given for security if necessary.

e. All that is needed for the building of a village for himself and his dependents shall be furnished them,—but as an interest bearing loan.

f. That he, and the colonists who will go with him, shall have full religious liberty, they being neither papists nor visionaries.

g. That if any of his dependents should fall into error no one should attempt to correct them, but leave him to handle the matter according to his own judgment; on the other hand he will stand surety for the conduct of his dependents as citizens.

h. That he and his descendents shall be taken under the protection of the English Nation if they request it.

i. That he may be permitted to choose whether he will go himself to Georgia, or send a representative to set his affairs in order, and if the latter, then the representative shall receive the courteous treatment that would have been accorded him.

j. That those among his colonists who wish to preach the gospel to the heathen shall be allowed to do so; and their converts shall have the same religious freedom as his colonists.

k. That he and his dependents in Georgia shall be given the privileges in spiritual affairs which the independent Lords of Germany enjoy in temporal affairs.

l. That all his property shall be at the service of

the State in time of need, but neither he nor his dependents shall be called on for military duty, in lieu whereof he will, if necessary, pay a double war tax."

From this document it appears that even at this early stage of the negotiations Zinzendorf's plans for the settlement in Georgia were well matured. A town was to be built by his colonists, where they should have all privileges for the free exercise of their religion; they, as thrifty citizens, were to assist in the upbuilding of Georgia; they were to preach the gospel to the heathen; they were *not* to bear arms, but in case of war to pay a double tax. His careful avoidance of the plea of religious persecution was caused by the fact that his own King had ordered the exile of the Schwenkfelders, for Zinzendorf all his life sought to pay due respect to those in authority, and even when his conscience forced him to differ with them it was done with perfect courtesy, giving equal weight to all parts of the commandment "Honor all men; love the brotherhood; fear God; honor the King."

The proposals of the Count were forwarded through Herr von Pfeil, and were presented to the Trustees of the Colony of Georgia by a Mr. Lorenz. Who this gentleman was does not appear, but a man bearing that name was one of the Germans, living in London, who in 1737 formed a society for religious improvement under the influence of Count Zinzendorf.

Through the same channel the answer of the Trustees was returned:

"Mr. Lorenz,

The proposals sent by Baron Pfeil from Ratisbon (Regensberg) to the Trustees of Georgia have been read at their meeting, but as they see that the gentleman asks pecuniary assistance for the establishment he contemplates, they answer that they have absolutely no fund from which to defray such expenses, but that in case the gentleman who suggests it wishes to undertake the enterprise at his own cost they will be able to grant him land in Georgia on conditions to which no one could object, and which he may learn as soon as the Trustees have been informed that he has decided to go at his own expense. You will have the kindness to forward this to Baron Pfeil, and oblige,

your most humble

servant J. Vernon."

Whether this plea of "no fund" was prompted by indifference, or whether they really considered the money appropriated by Parliament as intended for the Salzburgers alone, is immaterial. Perhaps Zinzendorf's very proposals to consider any assistance as a loan made them think him able to finance the scheme himself.

The Schwenkfelders, being under orders to expatriate themselves, left Berthelsdorf on the 26th of May, 1734, under the leadership of Christopher Wiegner (sometimes called George in Moravian MSS.) and at their request George Böhnisch, one of the Herrnhut Moravians, went with them. Their plan was to go through Holland to England, and thence to Georgia, but in the former country they changed their minds and sailed for Pennsylvania. In December of the same year Spangenberg was in Rotterdam, where he lodged with a Dr. Koker, from whom he learned the reason for their, until then, unexplained behavior. Dr. Koker belonged to a Society calling themselves the "Collegiants," the membership of which was drawn from the Reformed, Lutheran, and various other churches. Their cardinal principles were freedom of speech, freedom of belief, and liberty to retain membership in their own denominations if they desired. The Society was really an offshoot of the Baptist Church, differing, however, in its non-insistance upon a particular form of baptism. Twice a year the members met in the Lord's Supper, to which all were welcomed whose life was beyond reproach. In Holland they enjoyed the same privileges as other sects, and had a following in Amsterdam, Haarlem, Rotterdam, Leyden, etc.

It appeared that the Schwenkfelders had first addressed themselves to these Collegiants, especially to Cornelius van Putten in Haarlem, and Pieter Koker in Rotterdam, but when their need grew more pressing they appealed to Count Zinzendorf. When he was not able to obtain for them all they wanted, they turned again to the Collegiants, and were in conference with them in Rotterdam. The Collegiants were very much opposed to the Georgia Colony,—"the Dutch intensely disliked anything that would connect them with England,"—and although Thomas Coram, one of the Trustees, who happened to be in Rotterdam, promised the Schwenkfelders free transportation (which had been refused Zinzendorf), the Collegiants persuaded them not to go to Georgia. Their chief argument was that the English Government sent its convicts to Georgia, a proof that it was not a good land, and the Schwenkfelders were also told that the English intended to use them as slaves.

Disturbed by this view of the case, the Schwenkfelders accepted an offer of free transportation to Pennsylvania, where they arrived in safety on the 22nd of September.

Spangenberg had wished to serve as their pastor in Georgia, thinking it would give him opportunity to carry out his cherished wish to bear the gospel message to the heathen, and he felt himself still in a measure bound to them, despite their change of purpose, and at a somewhat later time did visit them in their new home. There was some idea of then taking them to Georgia, but it did not materialize, and they remained permanently in Pennsylvania, settling in the counties of Montgomery, Berks and Lehigh. Their descendents there preserve the customs of their fathers, and are the only representatives of the Schwenkfelder form of doctrine, the sect having become extinct in Europe.

PRELIMINARY STEPS.

While the exile of the Schwenkfelders was the immediate cause which led Zinzendorf to open negotiations with the Trustees of the Colony of Georgia, the impulse which prompted him involved far more than mere assistance to them. Foreign Missions, in the modern sense of the word, were almost unknown in Zinzendorf's boyhood, yet from his earliest days his thoughts turned often to those who lay beyond the reach of gospel light. In 1730, while on a visit to Copenhagen, he heard that the Lutheran Missionary Hans Egede, who for years had been laboring single handed to convert the Eskimos of Greenland, was sorely in need of help; and Anthony, the negro body-servant of a Count Laurwig, gave him a most pathetic description of the condition of the negro slaves in the Danish West Indies.

Filled with enthusiasm, Zinzendorf returned to Herrnhut, and poured the two stories into willing ears, for ever since the great revival of 1727 the Moravian emigrants had been scanning the field, anxious to carry the "good news" abroad, and held back only by the apparent impossibility of going forward. Who were they, without influence, without means, without a country even, that they should take such an office upon themselves? But the desire remained, and at this summons they prepared to do the impossible. In August, 1732, two men started for St. Thomas,—in April, 1733, three more sailed for Greenland, and in the face of hardships that would have daunted men of less than heroic mold, successful missions were established at both places.

But this was not enough. "My passionate desire," wrote Zinzendorf from Herrnhut in January, 1735, "my passionate desire to make Jesus known among the heathen has found a satisfaction in the blessed Greenland, St. Thomas and Lapp work, but without appeasing my hunger. I therefore look into every opportunity which presents itself, seeking that the kingdom of my Redeemer may be strengthened among men."

Nor did he lack ready assistants, for the Moravians were as eager as he. "When we in Herrnhut heard of Georgia, of which much was being published in the newspapers, and when we realized the opportunity it would give to carry the Truth to the heathen, several Brethren, who had the Lord's honor much at heart, were led, doubtless by His hand, to think that it would be a good plan to send some Brethren thither, if it might please the Lord to bless our work among the heathen, and so to bring those poor souls, now far from Christ, nigh unto Him. We tried to learn about the land, but could secure no accurate information, for some spoke from hearsay, others with prejudice, and many more with too great partiality. But we at last decided to venture, in the faith that the Lord would help us through."

The needs of the Schwenkfelders gave a new turn to their thoughts, and suggested the advantages that might accrue from a settlement in America to which they might all retreat if the persecution in Saxony waxed violent; but early in the year 1734, the question "Shall we go to Georgia only as Colonists, or also as Missionaries?" was submitted to the lot, and the answer was "As Missionaries also."

The defection of the Schwenkfelders, therefore, while a serious interference with the Herrnhut plan, was not allowed to ruin the project. Zinzendorf wrote again to the Trustees, and they repeated their promise of land, provided his colonists would go at their own expense.

After much consultation the decision was reached that Zinzendorf should ask for a tract of five hundred acres, and that ten men should be sent over to begin a town, their families and additional settlers to follow them in a few months.

The next step was to find a way to send these men across the Atlantic. Baron George Philipp Frederick von Reck, a nephew of Herr von Pfeil, who had led the first company of Salzburgers to Georgia, was planning to take a second company in the course of the next months. He was young and enthusiastic, met Zinzendorf's overtures most kindly, and even visited Herrnhut in the early part of October, 1734, when, as it happened, nine of the prospective colonists were formally presented to the Congregation. Baron Reck was very much impressed, promised to take with him to Georgia any of the Moravians who wished to go, and even sent to David Nitschmann, who was to conduct the party as far as London, full authorization to bring as many as desired to come, promising each man who went at his own expense a fifty-acre freehold in Georgia, and offering others necessary assistance when they reached London. This paper was signed at Bautzen, October 22nd, 1734.

But Reck had failed to realize the force of the Halle opposition to Herrnhut, and soon weakened under the weight of persuasion and command laid upon him by those whose opinion he felt obliged to respect. On the 4th of November he wrote from Windhausen to Graf Stolberg Wernigerode, "I have hesitated and vexed myself in much uncertainty whether or not I should go with the Herrnhuters to America. And now I know that God has heard our prayer at Halle and Wernigerode, and your letters have decided me to stay in Germany this winter, in the first place because my going would be a grief to my dear Urlsperger, whom I love as a father, secondly because the English will send over a third transport of Salzburgers in the coming spring and wish me to take them, and thirdly because I wish to obey worthy and chosen men of God."

He wrote to the same effect to Zinzendorf, and the Count, though doubtless annoyed, replied simply: "Your Highness' resolution to accomodate yourself to your superiors would be known by us all for right. You will then not blame us if we go our way as it is pointed out to us by the Lord."

A few days later Reck received a sharp note from the Trustees of Georgia, reproving him for his temerity in agreeing to take the Moravians with him to Georgia without consulting them, and reiterating the statement that the funds in their hands had been given for the use of the Salzburgers, and could be used for them alone.

The young man must have winced not a little under all this censure, but while he yielded his plan to the wishes of the Halle party, he held firmly to the opinion he had formed of the Moravians. He wrote to Urlsperger and others in their behalf, declaring that they were a godly people, much misunderstood, that it was a shame to persecute them and try to hinder their going to Georgia, and he felt sure that if their opponents would once meet the

Moravians and converse with them freely, confidentially, and without prejudice, they would come to respect them as he did. He also suggested that there were many protestants remaining in Bohemia, who would gladly leave, and who might be secured for Georgia on the terms offered to the Salzburgers. The next year in fact, an effort was made to obtain permission from the Austrian Government for the emigration of these people, and Reck was authorized by the Trustees to take them to Georgia, but nothing came of it.

Nor did his championship of the Bohemians and Moravians already in Saxony have any result. Urlsperger was offended that the negotiations from Herrnhut with the Trustees were not being carried on through him, "the only one in Germany to whom the Trustees had sent formal authority to receive people persecuted on account of religion, or forced to emigrate," and the Halle party were unable or unwilling to meet the leaders of the Moravians "without prejudice." The company of Salzburgers therefore sailed for Georgia in November without Baron von Reck, and without the Moravians, Mr. Vat acting as Commissary.

The Moravians, meanwhile, were not waiting idly for matters to turn their way, but even before Reck reached his decision Spangenberg had started for England to arrange personally with the Georgia Trustees for their emigration.

August Gottlieb Spangenberg was born July 15th, 1704, at Klettenberg, Prussia. In the year 1727, while a student at Jena, he became acquainted with the Moravians through a visit of two of their number, which won them many friends at that institution. Later, when he was Assistant Professor of Theology at Halle, he was required to sever his connection with the Moravians, or leave the University, and choosing the latter he came to Herrnhut in the spring of 1733. He was one of the strongest, ablest, and wisest leaders that the Unitas Fratrum has ever had, and eventually became a Bishop of the Unity, and a member of its governing board. He was a writer of marked ability, and in his diaries was accustomed to speak of himself as "Brother Joseph," by which name he was also widely known among the Moravians.

Spangenberg left Herrnhut in the late summer or early fall of 1734, bearing with him Zinzendorf's Power of Attorney to receive for him a grant from the Georgia Trustees of five hundred acres of land, and to transact all other necessary business. He stopped for some time in Holland, where he made a number of acquaintances, some of whom gave him letters of introduction to friends in England and in America, and others contributed toward the necessary expenses of the emigrants. From Rotterdam he wrote to Zinzendorf, saying that he heard no ship would sail for America before February or March, and that he thought it would be best for the colonists to wait until he wrote from London, and then to come by way of Altona, as the Holland route was very expensive. These suggestions, however, came too late, as the party had left Herrnhut before the arrival of his letter.

Spangenberg had a stormy voyage to England,

and on reaching London, rented a room in "Mr. Barlow's Coffee House, in Wattling's street, near St. Anthelius Church." He found the outlook rather discouraging, and a long letter written on the 10th of January, gives a vivid picture of the English mind regarding the "Herrnhuters." Spangenberg had called on several merchants to see if he could arrange a loan for the Moravians, for Zinzendorf's means were already strained to the utmost by what he was doing for the Church, and he did not see how it was possible to provide the money in any other way. But the merchants declined to make the loan, saying: "We can not take the land (in Georgia) as surety, for it is not yet settled, and no man would give us a doit for it; the personal security (of the emigrants) is also not sufficient, for they might all die on the sea or in Georgia,—there is danger of it, for the land is warmer than Europeans can bear, and many who have moved thither have died; if they settle on the land and then die the land reverts to the Trustees, so we would lose all; and the six per cent interest offered is not enough, for the money applied to business would yield twenty per cent.

Others objected to having the Moravians go at all especially Court Preacher Ziegenhagen, who belonged to the Halle party, and who, Spangenberg found, had much influence on account of his good judgment and spotless character. They claimed: (1) That the Moravians were not oppressed in Saxony, and had no good reason for wishing to leave; (2) that to say they wished to be near the heathen was only an excuse, for Georgia had nothing to do with the West Indies where they had a mission; (3) the Moravians could not bear the expense, and neither the Trustees nor the Society for the Propagation of Christian Knowledge would help them; (4) they could neither speak nor understand English, and would therefore be unable to support themselves in an English colony; (5) their going would create confusion, for Herr Bolzius, the pastor of the Salzburgers at Ebenezer, had written to beg that they should not be allowed to come; (6) if they went it would involve England in trouble with Saxony, and the Georgia Colony was not meant to take other rulers' subjects away from them, only to furnish an asylum for exiles, and poor Englishmen; (7) the Moravians could not remain subject to Zinzendorf, for they must all become naturalized Englishmen; (8) the suggestion that Zinzendorf's land could be cultivated by the heathen was absurd, for slavery was not permitted in Georgia and the Moravians could not afford to hire them; (9) ten or fifteen men, as were said to be on the way, would never be able to make headway in settling the forest, a task which had been almost too much for the large company of Salzburgers.

Some of these statements dealt with facts, about which the critics might have acquired better information, had they so desired, others were prophecies of which only the years to come could prove or disprove the truth, others again touched difficulties which were even then confronting Count Zinzendorf's agent; but in the light of contemporary writings and later developments, it is possible to glance at each point and see in how far the Halle party were

NEGOTIATIONS WITH TRUSTEES OF GEORGIA. 45

justified in their argument. (1) The treatment in Saxony, while not as yet a persecution which threatened them with torture and death, had many unpleasant features, and the constant agitation against them might at any time crystalize into harsh measures, for those members of the Herrnhut community who had left friends and relatives in the homelands of Bohemia and Moravia were already forbidden to invite them to follow, or even to receive them if they came unasked seeking religious freedom. (2) There was no idea of associating the missions in Georgia and the West Indies, for the heathen whom they wished to reach by this new settlement were the Creek and Cherokee Indians with whom Governor Oglethorpe had already established pleasant relations, bringing several of their chiefs to England, and sending them home filled with admiration for all they had seen, much impressed by the kindness shown them, and willing to meet any efforts that might be made to teach them. (3) The money question was a vital one, and it was principally to solve that that Spangenberg had come to England, where with Oglethorpe's help he later succeeded in securing the desired loan. (4) That they could speak little English was also a real difficulty; Spangenberg used Latin in his conferences with the educated men he met in London, but that medium was useless in Georgia, and while the Moravians learned English as rapidly as they could, and proved their capability for self-support, the failure to fully understand or be understood by their neighbors was responsible for many of the trials that were awaiting them in the New World. (5) The protest of Bolzius was only a part of the general Salzburger opposition, and to avoid friction in Georgia, Zinzendorf had particularly recommended that the Moravians settle in a village apart by themselves, where they could "lead godly lives, patterned after the writings and customs of the apostles," without giving offense to any; and he promised, for the same reason, that as soon as they were established he would send them a regularly ordained minister, although laymen were doing missionary work in other fields. (6) In order to avoid any danger of creating trouble between the Governments, the Moravian colonists carefully said nothing in London regarding their difficulties in Saxony, or the persecutions in Bohemia and Moravia, and instead of proclaiming themselves exiles for the Faith as they might have done with perfect truth, they appeared simply as Count Zinzendorf's servants, sent by him to cultivate the five hundred acres about to be given to him, and by his orders to preach to the Indians. (7) A change of nationality would not affect the relation between Zinzendorf and his colonists, for their position as his dependents in Germany was purely voluntary, such service as they rendered was freely given in exchange for his legal protection, and his supremacy in Church affairs then and later was a recognition of the personal character of the man, not a yielding of submission to the Count. (8) That the Indians could not be employed on Zinzendorf's estate was quite true, not so much on account of the law against slavery, for the Count intended nothing of that kind, but their character and wild habits rendered them incapable of becoming good farmers, as the American Nation has learned through many years of effort and failure. (9) Whether the ten or fifteen men, reinforced by those who followed them, would have been able to make a home in the heart of the forest, will never be known, for from various reasons the town on the five hundred acre tract was never begun. In short, while the Moravians were risking much personal discomfort, there was nothing in their plan which could possibly injure others, and the cavil and abuse of their opposers was as uncalled for as is many a "private opinion publicly expressed" to-day.

Hearing of the many obstacles which were being thrown in their way, Mr. Coram, who was a man of wide charities, and interested in other colonies besides Georgia, suggested to Spangenberg that his company should go to Nova Scotia, where the climate was milder, and offered them free transportation and aid in settling there, but this proposal Spangenberg at once rejected, and pinned his faith on the kindness of Gen. Oglethorpe, whose return from Georgia the preceding July, explained the more favorable tone of the Trustees' letters after that date. Oglethorpe asked him numberless questions about the doctrine and practice of the Moravians, and their reasons for wishing to go to Georgia, and promised to lay the matter before the Trustees, using all his influence to further their designs.

THE "FIRST COMPANY."

On the 14th of January, 1735, the first company

of Moravian colonists arrived in London. At their head was David Nitschmann,—variously called "the III," "the weaver," "the Syndic," and Count Zinzendorf's "Hausmeister," who was to stay with them until they left England, and then return to Germany, resigning the leadership of the party to Spangenberg, who was instructed to take them to Georgia and establish them there, and then go to Pennsylvania to the Schwenkfelders. The other nine were

    John Töltschig, Zinzendorf's flower-gardener.
    Peter Rose, a gamekeeper.
    Gotthard Demuth, a joiner.
    Gottfried Haberecht, weaver of woolen goods.
    Anton Seifert, a linen weaver.
    George Waschke, carpenter.
    Michael Haberland, carpenter.
    George Haberland, mason.
    Friedrich Riedel, mason.

They were " good and true sons of God, and at the same time skillful workmen," with such a variety of handicrafts as to render them largely independent of outside assistance in the settlement which they proposed to make; and all but Haberecht were religious refugees from Moravia and adjacent parts of Bohemia.

Nitschmann and Töltschig were two of the five young men in Zauchenthal, Moravia, who had set their hearts on the revival of the ancient Unitas Fratrum. Töltschig's father, the village burgess, had summoned the five comrades before him, and strictly forbidden their holding religious services, warning them that any attempt at emigration would be severely punished, and advising them to act as became their youth, frequent the taverns and take part in dances and other amusements. They were sons of well-to-do parents, and little more than boys in years, (Nitschmann was only twenty), but their faith and purpose were dearer to them than anything else on earth, so they had left all and come away, commending their homes and kindred to the mercy of God, and singing the exile hymn of the ancient Unitas Fratrum, sacred through its association with those brave hearts who had known the bitterness and the joy of exile a hundred years before.

" Blessed the day when I must go
My fatherland no more to know,
  My lot the exile's loneliness;

" For God will my protector be,
And angels ministrant for me
  The path with joys divine will bless.

" And God to some small place will guide
Where I may well content abide
  And where this soul of mine may rest.

"As thirsty harts for water burn,
For Thee, my Lord and God, I yearn,
  If Thou are mine my life is blest."

Though holding positions as Count Zinzendorf's hausmeister and gardener, both Nitschmann and Töltschig were actively employed in the affairs of the renewed Unitas Fratum, and had been to England in 1728 to try to establish relations with the Society for the Propagation of Christian Knowledge, though without success. They were the better fitted, therefore, to conduct the party to England, and to share in the negotiations already begun by Spangenberg.

This "first company" left Herrnhut on the 21st of November, 1734, traveling by Ebersdorf (where Henry XXIX, Count Reuss, Countess Zinzendorf's brother, gave them a letter of recommendation to any whom they might meet on their way), to Holland, whence they had a stormy and dangerous voyage to England.

The day after they reached London they called on Gen. Oglethorpe and having gained admittance with some difficulty they were very well received by him, carrying on a conversation in a mixture of English and German, but understanding each other fairly well. Spangenberg coming in most opportunely, the Moravian affairs were fully discussed, and the new-comers learned that their arrival had been fortunately timed, for the Georgia Trustees were to hold one of their semi-annual meetings two days later, when Oglethorpe could press their matter, and a ship was to sail for Georgia the latter part of the month. Oglethorpe was disturbed to find that the colonists had failed to raise any money toward their expenses, but promised to try and assist them in that also.

On the 18th the colonists were formally presented to the Trustees, heard the lively argument for and against their cause, and had the satisfaction

GENERAL OGLETHORPE.

NEGOTIATIONS WITH TRUSTEES OF GEORGIA. 51

of seeing the vote cast in their favor. It was contrary to the custom of the Trustees to grant lands to any who did not come in person to apply for them and declare their intention of going to Georgia to settle, but Oglethorpe's argument that the high rank of Count Zinzendorf was entitled to consideration was accepted and five hundred acres of land were granted to the Count and his male heirs.

The Indenture bore date of Jan. 10, 1734, Old Style, (Jan. 21, 1735,) and the five hundred acres were "to be set out limited and bounded in Such Manner and in Such Part or Parts of the said Province as shall be thought most convenient by such Person or Persons as shall by the said Common Council be for that Purpose authorized and appointed," there being a verbal agreement that the tract should be in the hilly country some distance from the coast, which, though less accessible and less easily cultivated, lay near the territory occupied by the Indians. Five pounds per annum was named as the quit rent, payment to begin eight years later; and such part of the tract as was not cleared and improved during the next eighteen years was to revert to the Trustees. The Trustees also agreed that they would reserve two hundred acres near the larger tract, and whenever formally requested by Count Zinzendorf, would grant twenty acres each "to such able bodied Young Men Servants as should arrive and settle with him in the said Province of Georgia."

In addition to the five hundred acres granted to Zinzendorf, fifty acres were given to Spangenberg, and fifty acres to Nitschmann, although as the latter was not going to Georgia, and the former did not intend to stay, this alone was a departure from the custom of the Trustees. Each of the fifty acre grants was in three parts, a lot in the town of Savannah, a five acre garden, and a forty-five acre farm, and while their acquisition had not been a part of the Herrnhut plan the colonists readily yielded to the advice of their English friends, who pointed out the necessity of having a place to stay when they reached Savannah, and land that they could at once begin to cultivate, without waiting for the selection and survey of the larger tract. In fact, though they knew it not, these two grants, which lay side by side, were destined to be the scene of all their experiences in the Province of Georgia.

The Trustees seem to have been pleased with the appearance of their new settlers, and approved of their taking passage in the ship that was to sail the latter part of the month. Since the vessel had been chartered by the Trustees they promised to make no charge for such baggage as the Moravians wished to take with them, arranged that they should have a portion of the ship for themselves instead of being quartered with the other passengers, and offered Spangenberg a berth in the Captain's cabin. This he declined, preferring to share equally with his Brethren in the hardships of the voyage. Medicine was put into his hands to be dispensed to those who might need it, and he was requested to take charge of about forty Swiss emigrants who wished to go in the same vessel on their way to Purisburg in South Carolina, where they sought better material conditions than they had left at home.

Land having been secured, Gen. Oglethorpe arranged that the Trustees should lend the "First Company," £60, payable in five years, with the understanding that if repaid within that time the interest should be remitted, otherwise to be charged at ten per cent., the usual rate in South Carolina. Of this £10 was spent in London for supplies, and £50 paid their passage across the Atlantic. The ten men (Spangenberg taking Nitschmann's place) pledged themselves jointly and severally to the payment of the debt, the bond being signed on Jan. 22nd, (Jan. 11th, O. S.) the day after the grant of the land.

In addition to this Oglethorpe collected £26:5:0, as a gift for the Moravians, £10 being presented to them in cash in London, and the rest forwarded to Savannah with instructions that they should be supplied with cattle, hogs and poultry to that amount. Oglethorpe further instructed Messrs. Toojesiys and Baker, of Charlestown, to honor Spangenberg's drafts on him to the amount of £20, so securing the settlers against possible need in their new home.

The next day Gen. Oglethorpe presented Spangenberg to the Bishop of London, who received him very kindly. Oglethorpe's idea was that the Moravians might ally themselves closely with the Church of England, and that the Bishop might, if they wished, ordain one of their members from Herrnhut. Spangenberg and Nitschmann were not authorized to enter into any such agreement, but both welcomed the opportunity to establish pleasant relations with the English clergy, and several interviews were had which served as a good opening for intercourse in later years.

Until their vessel sailed, the Moravians found plenty to interest them in the "terribly great city," where they were regarded with much interest, and where they were greatly touched by the unexpected kindness they received.

They had interviews with the Trustees, with Mr. Vernon, and with Gen. Oglethorpe, who gave them much information as to what to expect in their new home, and many suggestions as to the best way of beginning their settlement. Spangenberg was presented to the "Society for the Propagation of Christian Knowledge," was courteously received, offered more books than he was willing to accept, invited to correspond with the Society, and urged to keep on friendly terms with the Salzburgers, which he assured them he sincerely desired to do. Conversations with Court--Preacher Ziegenhagen were not so pleasant, for a letter had come from Senior Urlsperger inveighing against the Moravians and Ziegenhagen put forth every effort to reclaim Spangenberg from the supposed error of his ways, and to persuade him to stop the company about to start for Georgia, or at least to separate himself from them, and return to the old friends at Halle. Oglethorpe smiled at the prejudice against the Moravians, and told them frankly that efforts had been made to influence him, but he had preferred to wait and judge for himself. "It has ever been so," he said, "from the time of the early Christians; it seems to be the custom of theologians to call others heretics. They say, in short, 'you do not believe what I believe, a Mohammedan also does not believe what I believe, therefore you are a Mohammedan;' and again 'you explain this Bible passage so and so, the Socinian also explains it so and so, therefore you are a Socinian.'" As for opposition, he, too, was beginning to find it since the Georgia Colony was proving a success.

Meanwhile new friends were springing up on every side of the Moravians. A doctor helped them lay in a store of medicine, another gave them some balsam which was good for numberless external and internal uses. A German merchant, who had become an English citizen, helped them purchase such things as they would require in Georgia, and a cobbler assisted Riedel in buying a shoemaker's outfit. Weapons were offered to all the members of the party, but declined, as they wished to give no excuse to any one who might try to press them into military service. They yielded, however, to the argument that they would need to protect themselves against wolves and bears, and sent Peter Rose, the gamekeeper, with Mr. Verelst, one of the secretaries of the Trustees, to purchase a fowling piece and hunting knives.

Letters of introduction to various prominent men in America were given to them; and, perhaps most important of all in its future bearing, people discovered the peculiar charm of the Moravian services. Reference is made in the diaries to one and another,—from English clergyman to Germans resident in London,—who joined with them in their devotions, and seemed much moved thereby. Neither was it a passing emotion, for the seed a little later blossomed into the English Moravian Church.

And so the month passed swiftly by, and the ship was ready to commence her long voyage.

CHAPTER III.

THE FIRST YEAR IN GEORGIA.

THE VOYAGE.

In the year 1735 a voyage across the Atlantic was a very different thing from what it is in this year of grace 1904. To-day a mighty steamship equipped with powerful engines, plows its way across the billows with little regard for wind and weather, bearing thousands of passengers, many of whom are given all the luxury that space permits, a table that equals any provided by the best hotels ashore, and attendance that is unsurpassed. Then weeks were consumed in the mere effort to get away from the British Isles, the breeze sometimes permitting the small sailing vessels to slip from one port to another, and then holding them prisoner for days before another mile could be gained. Even the most aristocratic voyager was forced to be content with accommodations and fare little better than that supplied to a modern steerage passenger, and those who could afford it took with them a private stock of provisions to supplement the ship's table.

And yet the spell of adventure or philanthropy, gain or religion, was strong upon the souls of men, and thousands sought the New World, where their imagination saw the realization of all their dreams. Bravely they crossed the fathomless deep which heaved beneath them, cutting them off so absolutely from the loved ones left at home, from the wise counsels of those on whom they were accustomed to depend, and from the strong arm of the Government under whose promised protection they sailed, to work out their own salvation in a country where each man claimed to be a law unto himself, and where years were to pass before Experience had once more taught the lesson that real freedom was to be gained only through a general recognition of the rights of others.

On the 3rd of February, 1735, the Moravians arose early in their London lodging house, prayed heartily together, and then prepared to go aboard their vessel, "The Two Brothers," Capt. Thomson, where the Trustees wished to see all who intended to sail on her. A parting visit was paid to Gen. Oglethorpe, who presented them with a hamper of wine, and gave them his best wishes. After the review on the boat Spangenberg and Nitschmann returned with Mr. Vernon to London to attend to some last matters, while the ship proceeded to Gravesend for her supply of water, where Spangenberg rejoined her a few days later. On the 25th of February they passed the Azores, and disembarked at Savannah, April 8th, having been nine and a half weeks on shipboard.

The story of those nine weeks is simply, but graphically, told in the diary sent back to Herrnhut. Scarcely had they lifted anchor when the Moravians began to arrange their days, that they might not be idly wasted. In Herrnhut it was customary to divide the twenty-four hours among several members of the Church, so that night and day a continuous stream of prayer and praise arose to the throne of God, and the same plan was now adopted, with the understanding that when sea-sickness overtook the company, and they were weak and ill, no time limit should be fixed for the devotions of any, but one man should pass the duty to another as circumstances required!

Other arrangements are recorded later, when, having grown accustomed to ship life, they sought additional means of grace. In the early morning, before the other passengers were up, the Moravians gathered on deck to hold a service of prayer; in the afternoon much time was given to Bible reading; and in the evening hymns were sung that bore on the text that had been given in the morning. Spangenberg, Töltschig, and Seifert, in the order named, were the recognized leaders of the party, but realizing that men might journey together, and live together, and still know each other only superficially, it was agreed that each of the ten in turn should on successive days speak to every one of his brethren face to face and heart to heart. That there might be no confusion, two were appointed to bring the food to the company at regular times, and see that it was properly served, the following being "the daily Allowance of Provisions to the Passengers on board the "Two Brothers," Captain William Thomson, for the Town of Savannah in Georgia.

"On the four beef-days in each week for every mess of five heads (computing a head 12 years old, and under 12 two for one, and under 7 three for one, and under 2 not computed), 4 lbs. of beef and $2\frac{1}{2}$ lbs. of flour, and $\frac{1}{2}$ lb. of plums.

"On the two pork days in each week for said mess, 5 lbs. of pork and 2½ pints of peas.

"And on the fish day in each week for said mess, 2½ lbs. of fish and ½ lb. of butter.

"The whole at 16 ounces to the pound.

"And allow each head 7 lbs. of bread, of 14 ounces to the pound, by the week.

"And 3 pints of beer, and 2 quarts of water (whereof one of the quarts for drinking), each head by the day for the space of a month.

"And a gallon of water (whereof two quarts for drinking) each head, by the day after, during their being on their Passage."

Another Moravian was chosen as nurse of the company, although it happened at least once that he was incapacitated, for every man in the party was sick except Spangenberg, who was a capital sailor, and not affected by rough weather. His endurance was severely tested too, for while the breeze at times was so light that they unitedly prayed for wind, "thinking that the sea was not their proper element, for from the earth God had made them, and on the earth He had work for them to do," at other times storms broke upon them and waves swept the decks, filling them with awe, though not with fear. "The wind was high, the waves great, we were happy that we have a Saviour who would never show us malice; especially were we full of joy that we had a witness in our hearts that it was for a pure purpose we sailed to Georgia,"—so runs the quaint record of one tempestuous day.

A more poetic expression of the same thought is given by Spangenberg in a poem written during the voyage, and sent home to David Nitschmann to be set to the music of some "Danish Melody" known to them both. There is a beauty of rythm in the original which the English cannot reproduce, as though the writer had caught the cadence of the waves, on some bright day when the ship "went softly" after a season of heavy storm.

"Gute Liebe, deine Triebe
  Zünden unsre Triebe an,
Dir zu leben, dir zu geben,
  Was ein Mensch dir geben kann;
Denn dein Leben, ist, zu geben
  Fried' und Segen aus der Höh.
Und das Kränken zu versenken
  In die ungeheure See.

"Herr wir waren von den Schaaren
  Deiner Schäflein abgetrennt;
Und wir liefen zu den Tiefen,
  Da das Schwefelfeuer brennt,
Und dein Herze brach vor Schmerze,
  Ueber unsern Jammerstand;
O wie liefst du! O wie riefst du!
  Bist du uns zu dir gewandt.

"Als die Klarheit deiner Wahrheit
  Unsern ganzen Geist durchgoss,
Und von deinen Liebesscheinen
  Unser ganzes Herz zerfloss,
O wie regte und bewegte
  Dieses deine Liebesbrust,
Uns zu hegen und zu pflegen,
  Bis zur süssen Himmelslust.

" Dein Erbarmen wird uns Armen,
　　Alle Tage wieder neu,
Mit was süssen Liebesküssen
　　Zeigst du deine Muttertreu.
O wie heilig und wie treulich
　　Leitest du dein Eigentum;
O der Gnaden dass wir Maden
　　Werden deine Kron' und Ruhm.

"Wir empfehlen unsre Seelen
　　Deinem Aug' und Herz und Hand,
Denn wir werden nur auf Erden
　　Wallen nach dem Vaterland.
O gieb Gnade auf dem Pfade,
　　Der zum Reich durch Leiden führt,
Ohn' Verweilen fortzueilen
　　Bis uns deine Krone ziert.

"Unser Wille bleibe stille
　　Wenn es noch so widrig geht;
Lass nur brausen, wüten, sausen,
　　Was von Nord und Osten weht.
Lass nur stürmen, lass sich türmen
　　Alle Fluthen aus dem See,
Du erblickest und erquickest
　　Deine Kinder aus der Höh'."

(Love Divine, may Thy sweet power
　　Lead us all for Thee to live,
And with willing hearts to give Thee
　　What to Thee a man can give;
For from heaven Thou dost give us

Peace and blessing, full and free,
And our miseries dost bury
In the vast, unfathomed sea.

Lord, our wayward steps had led us
Far from Thy safe-guarded fold,
As we hastened toward the darkness
Where the sulphurous vapors rolled;
And Thy kind heart throbbed with pity,
Our distress and woe to see,
Thou didst hasten, Thou didst call us,
Till we turned our steps to Thee.

As Thy Truth's convincing clearness
Filled our spirits from above,
And our stubborn hearts were melted
By the fervor of Thy love,
O Thy loving heart was moved
Us Thy righteous laws to teach,
Us to guide, protect and cherish
Till Thy heaven we should reach.

Without merit we, yet mercy
Each returning day doth bless
With the tokens of Thy goodness,
Pledges of Thy faithfulness.
O how surely and securely
Dost Thou lead and guard Thine own;
O what wonderous grace that mortals
May add lustre to Thy throne.

In our souls we feel the presence
Of Thine eye and heart and hand,

> As we here on earth as pilgrims
>   Journey toward the Fatherland.
> O give grace, that on the pathway,
>   Which through trial leads to heaven,
> Without faltering we may hasten
>   Till to each Thy crown is given.
>
> Though our path be set with danger
>   Nothing shall our spirits shake,
> Winds may rage and roar and whistle,
>   Storms from North and East may break,
> Waves may roll and leap and thunder
>   On a dark and threatening sea,
> Thou dost ever watch Thy children,
>   And their strength and peace wilt be.)

Before the vessel sailed the Trustees had followed up their request to Spangenberg by requiring the forty Swiss emigrants to promise submission to his authority, and consequently numerous efforts were made to be of service to them. It was disappointing work, in a way, for attempts to give them religious instruction were met with utter indifference, but their material needs were many. There was a great deal of sickness among them, and four died, being buried hastily, and without ceremony. The Moravians themselves were not exempt, several being dangerously ill at times, even Spangenberg was prostrated, from having, he supposed, stayed too long on deck in the night air, tempted thereto by the beauty of a calm night in a southern latitude. But having work to do among the Swiss on the following day, he roused himself, and soon became better. Two of the Moravians were appointed nurses for the sick Swiss, and by the use of the medicine provided by the Trustees, supplemented by unwearying personal attention, they were made as comfortable as possible.

Nor were the crew forgotten. From the day when the Moravians helped lift the anchor as they sailed from the coast of Dover, they busied themselves in the work of the ship, always obliging, always helpful, until the sailors came to trust them absolutely, "even with the keys to their lockers." When the cook was suddenly taken sick they nursed him carefully, and then appointed two of their number to carry wood and water for him until his strength returned, and it is no wonder that such accommodating passengers were well regarded.

Captain Thomson was disposed to favor them, but when they realized that they were receiving a larger share of food and drink than went to the Swiss, they courteously declined, fearing it would breed jealousy. His kindly feeling, however, continued, and when Töltschig was ill he brought a freshly killed fowl from which to make nourishing broth, and on another occasion, after a severe attack of seasickness, they all derived much benefit from some strong beer which he urged upon them.

There were a few cabin passengers on the ship, and on one occasion Spangenberg was invited to dine with them, but their light jesting was distasteful to him, and the acquaintance was not pursued.

MAKING A START.

The vessel entered the Savannah River, April 6th, and the Captain, taking Spangenberg and Töltschig into his small boat, went ahead to the town of Savannah, the capital of Georgia, now the home of about six hundred people. Spangenberg had a letter of introduction to Mr. Causton, who received him and his companion in a friendly fashion, entertained them at supper, and kept them over night. Mr. Causton was one of the three magistrates charged with all civil and criminal jurisdiction in Savannah, and his position as keeper of the Store, from which all provisions promised by the Trustees were dispensed, gave him such additional power that he was really the dictator of Savannah, ruling so absolutely that the people finally rebelled, and in 1738 secured his dismissal from office. On his return to England in 1739, he found great difficulty in trying to explain his accounts to the Trustees, was sent back to Georgia to procure some needed papers, died on the passage over, and was buried in the ocean. His treatment of the Moravians was characteristic, for he was courtesy itself to the new-comers who had money to spend, inconsiderate when hard times came, deaf to appeals for settlement of certain vexing questions, and harsh when their wills were opposed to his.

The next morning, before sunrise, Spangenberg and Töltschig went apart into the woods, fell upon their knees, and thanked the Lord that He had brought them hither in safety. The day was spent in gaining information as to the customs of the place, Mr. Causton again claiming them as his guests at dinner, and in the evening they accepted the invitation of a merchant to supper. As they ate, the report of a cannon announced the arrival of their

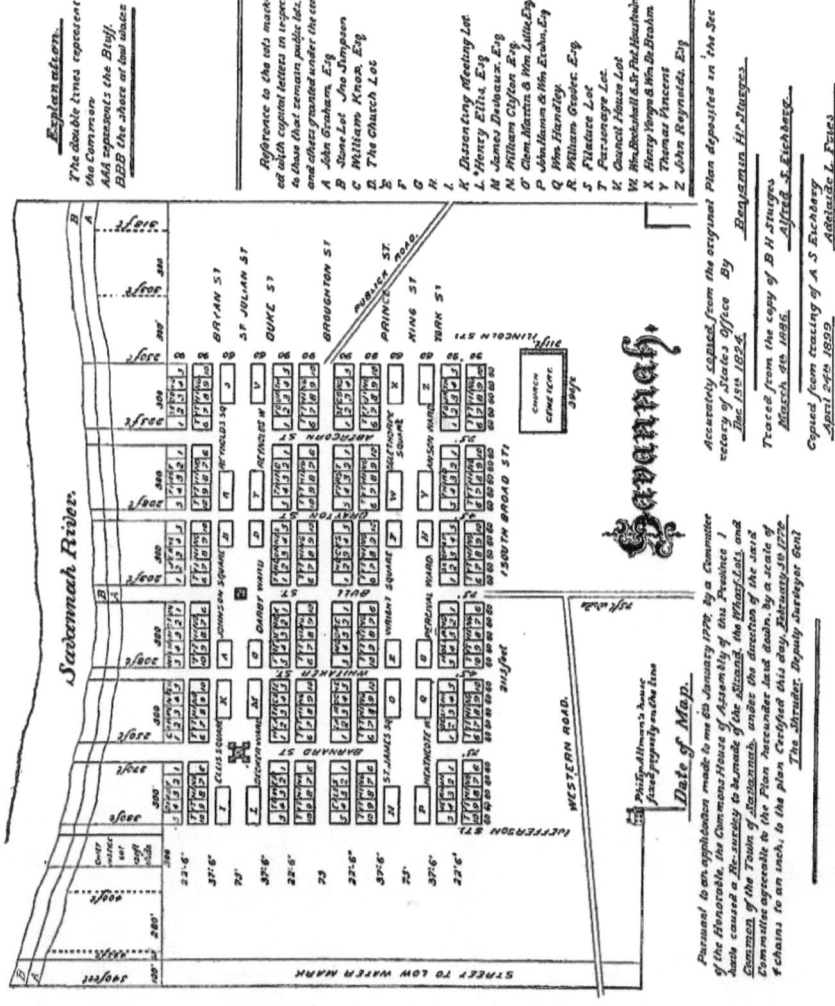

vessel, and Töltschig went to spend the night aboard, Spangenberg remaining on shore to push the preparation for the reception of the company.

Early on the following morning, April 8th, he had their town lots assigned, (Nos. 3 and 4 Second Tything, Anson Ward), in order that their baggage might be brought directly to their own property, for he had found that lodgings in the town were very dear, and decided that a small cabin should be built at once and a house as soon as possible. Going then to the ship he guided the company to their new home, and the entire day was consumed in moving their belongings to the town, as it was some distance, and everything had to be carried by hand to the little hut which was hastily erected and roofed over with sacking. Evening came before they had really finished the arrangement of their possesions, but before they prepared and shared their evening meal, they humbly knelt and thanked God for His mercies, discussed the Bible text for the day, and joined in several familiar hymns. A New York merchant stopped and asked them to sing one of his favorites, which was done, and an Indian who had joined them near the river and followed them home, stayed through the service, and at parting beckoned them to come and visit him. Despite their fatigue, the "Hourly Intercession" was observed throughout the night, their slumbers rendered more peaceful by the knowledge that one and another in turn was watching and praying beside them.

On the following day two more Indians visited the Moravians. Their faces were adorned with streaks of red paint, and they seemed very friendly, rejoiced over the gift of two pewter mugs, and on leaving made signs that some one should go with them, an invitation that could not then be accepted.

The 10th of April, the first Sunday in America, Spangenberg attended service in the English Church, and heard a sermon on the text, "Be not overcome of evil, but overcome evil with good," well fitted to be the watchword of the Moravian settlers in the trials that were before them.

No unpleasant presentiments, however, troubled them, as they went busily about their work during the next weeks. Mr. Causton was very pleasant to them, selling them provisions at cost, offering them credit at the store, and promising Spangenberg a list of such Indian words as he had been able to learn and write down. He also introduced him to Tomochichi, the Indian Chief, and to John Musgrove, who had a successful trading house near the town. Musgrove had married Mary, an Indian princess of the Uchees, who had great influence with all the neighboring tribes. At a later time, through the machinations of her third husband, she made much trouble in Georgia, but during the earlier years of the Colony she was the true friend of the white settlers, frequently acting as Interpreter in their conferences with the Indians, and doing much to make and keep the bond of peace between the two races.

On the 11th of April the five acre garden belonging to Spangenberg was surveyed, and work was immediately begun there, as it was just the season for planting corn. Nine days later Nitschmann's garden was laid out aside of Spangenberg's. By the 14th the cabin on Spangenberg's town lot was finished. It was twenty feet long, ten feet wide, and fourteen feet high, with a little loft where they slept, their goods, with a table and benches being in the room below. At daybreak they rose, sang a hymn, and prayed together, breakfasted at eight o'clock, the daily text being read aloud, then worked until half past eleven, when they dined and read the Bible. More work, an evening prayer service, and such conference as was needed that each might engage in the next day's labor to the best advantage, prepared them for their well-earned repose.

With this simple program steadily carried out, much was accomplished. A fence was built around a small kitchen-garden on their town property, and a chicken-yard was enclosed, while the neighbors came to look on and opine " that the Moravians had done more in a week than their people in two years." As the gardens (the five acre lots) lay at some distance from Savannah, a hut was built there, to serve as a shelter against sun and rain, a heavy storm having chased them home one day soon after their arrival.

Either from the noonday heat, or other conditions to which they were not yet acclimated, Gotthard Demuth and George Haberland became seriously ill, causing Spangenberg much anxiety, for he did not feel at liberty to send for a physician, as they could not afford to pay for medicine. So resort was had to bleeding, then an approved practice, and to such medicine as remained from their voyage, and Rose was fortunate enough to shoot a grouse, which gave them some much needed palatable meat and broth. Perhaps the most serious case was Gottfried Haberecht's, who suffered for several days with fever resulting from a cut on his leg. Finally oak-leaves were heated and bound about the limb, which induced free perspiration and quickly relieved him, so that he was able to return to work!

A day was appointed on which Spangenberg and several others were to ride out into the country to select the five hundred acre tract granted to Count Zinzendorf, and the additional two hundred acres which the Trustees had promised to hold in reserve, and grant to the Count's "servants" whenever he should request it, but there was rumor of a raid by hostile Indians, under Spanish influence, so the expedition had to be postponed, with the promise, however, that it should be made as soon as possible.

By the close of the third week in Georgia the invalids were better, and matters were in such a shape that the Moravians resolved "that on each Saturday work should stop early, and every Sunday should be a real day of rest." As an immediate beginning, they on Saturday evening united in a Lovefeast, where "we recalled much loving-kindness which God has shown us hitherto; Töltschig washed the feet of the Brethren; we remained together until very late, and were truly blessed."

AIM AND ATTAINMENT.

When the "first company" left Herrnhut for London and the New World, they took with them Count Zinzendorf's formal "Instructions" for the conduct of their affairs:

"I shall not attempt to tell you what you are to do from day to day. I know that in many ways Love will lead you, prepare the way, and point out your path. I shall only bid you remember the principles and customs of our Congregation, in which, if you stand fast, you will do well. Your one aim will be to establish a little place near the heathen where you may gather together the dispersed in Israel, patiently win back the wayward, and instruct the heathen tribes.

"You have and will ask nothing more than the opportunity to attain this end through your own labors, but you will request free transportation for yourselves and those who will follow you,—if they receive your present small number the Lord will send you more.

"If you should be tempted to injure any work of the Lord for my sake, refrain from doing it, remembering that I am under a gracious guardianship which nothing can disturb.

"You will take absolutely no part in the Spangenberg—Halle controversy; you know the mind of the Congregation regarding it. If you find people prejudiced against you leave it to Him who has bidden you go to Georgia. Enter into no disputes, but, if questions are asked, give the history of the Congregation, being careful not to censure our opposers, and saying, which is true, that the Congregation at Herrnhut gives them little heed. Entire freedom of conscience must be granted you, but there may be points which you can yield without injuring the cause of Christ,—if so you will find them in due time.

"You must live alone, establishing your own little corner, where your customs will irritate no one; and as soon as you are settled an ordained minister will be sent you, out of consideration for the scruples of the Salzburgers, although our Brethren in other Colonies are served by laymen, as permitted by our ancient constitution.

"God willing, I shall soon follow you, and only wait until He opens the way for me. Our dear Elder (Spangenberg) will quickly return from America, and in his absence I commit you to the mighty grace of God.

    Your brother and servant,
      Lewis Count v. Zinzendorf.

"At this time one of the Elders at Herrnhut. November 27th, 1734.

"'He everywhere hath way,
And all thing serve His might, etc.'"

That these sensible and liberal instructions were not fully carried out is at once apparent, especially in the two points of free transportation and settlement in a quiet, secluded spot. The inability of the Trustees to grant their request for the first, burdened the Moravian colonists with what was, under the circumstances, a heavy debt, while the location of Zinzendorf's five hundred acre tract was responsible for their failure in attaining the second.

When Gen. Oglethorpe planned the fortifications and defense of Savannah in 1733, he decided to erect a small fort on the Ogeechee River, some miles south, in order to command one of the trails by which the Indians had been accustomed to invade Carolina. This "Fort Argyle" was garrisoned with a detachment of rangers, and ten families were sent from Savannah to cultivate the adjacent land. The tract selected in London for Count Zinzendorf, was to lie on the Ogeechee, near Fort Argyle, an excellent place from which to reach the Indians in times of peace, but the worst possible location for non-combatants when war was threatening.

Spangenberg urged the survey of the five hundred acre tract as often and as strongly as he dared, but from various causes, chiefly rumors of Indian incursions, the expedition was deferred until Aug. 22nd, when Spangenberg, Töltschig, Riedel, Seifert, Rose, Michael Haberland, and Mr. Johnson, the Trustees' surveyor, prepared to start on their toilsome journey, going by boat, instead of attempting to follow the circuitous, ill-marked road across the country, impassable to pedestrians, though used to some extent by horsemen.

At one o'clock in the morning of Aug. 23rd the seven men embarked, taking advantage of the ebbing tide, and made their way down the Savannah River. It was very dark, the Moravians were unaccustomed to rowing, and Mr. Johnson, who steered, went to sleep time after time, so when they accidentally came across a ship riding at anchor they decided to stay by her and wait for the day. When dawn broke they hastened on to Thunderbolt, where a fort had been built, and some good land cleared, and there they found two Indians, who claimed to know the country, and agreed to go with them as pilots. Toward evening they reached Seituah,* where a stockade was being built as a protection against the Indians, and the night was spent with a Captain Wargessen (Ferguson), who, with several

---

*On Skidaway Island, exact site unknown.

soldiers, was out in a scout boat watching the movements of the Indians and Spaniards in that neighborhood.

The next day they made their way among the islands until they reached the mouth of the Ogeechee, up which they turned, but night overtook them, and they were forced to drop their anchor. The Indians had been left behind somewhere, and with the return of day it became necessary to retrace their course for some hours in order to learn where they were. That night was spent at Sterling's Bluff, with the Scotch who had settled upon it, and the next morning they proceeded to Fort Argyle. As they rowed up the river, a bear left one of the islands, and swam across to the main land. "He was better to us than we to him, for Peter shot at him twice when he came near us, but he left us in peace and went his way!"

The following morning Spangenberg and Johnson, accompanied by the Lieutenant from Fort Argyle and several of his rangers, rode out to inspect the land selected for the Moravians. The horses were accustomed to service against the Indians, and went at full gallop, pausing not for winding paths or fallen trees, and the University-bred man of Germany expected momentarily to have his neck broken, but nothing happened, and after looking over the tract they returned to Fort Argyle.

Despite the exertions of the morning Spangenberg then manned his boat, and started up the river to visit an Indian town, where he hoped to find Tomochichi. Much floating timber rendered the

trip dangerous and tedious, and it was not until early Sunday morning that they reached their destination, only to find the place deserted, as the band had left a few days before for a hunting expedition, and, if fortune favored them, for a brush with the Spanish Indians, with whom they had a perpetual feud. Soon Johnson appeared, guided by some of the rangers, who, after a hearty meal with the Moravians, returned to the Fort, Johnson remaining behind.

Monday morning, August 29th, before the sun rose, the party repaired to the Moravian tract, which Johnson surveyed, the Moravians acting as chain-carriers. Spangenberg was much pleased with the tract. It had a half mile frontage on the Ogeechee, extended two miles back into the forest, and gave a good variety of land, some low and damp for the cultivation of rice, sandy soil covered with grass for pasturage, and dry uplands suitable for corn and vegetables. A rapid stream furnished an abundance of pure water, and site for a mill, while the thick growth of timber guaranteed a supply of material for houses and boats. Near the river rose a high hill, where it had once been the intention to build a fort, and a house had really been erected. This the Indians burned, and later another site had been chosen for Fort Argyle, but the place retained the name of "Old Fort," and the hill would serve as the location for the Moravian dwelling.

Indian tribes which were friendly to the English lived at no great distance, and the trail to Savannah and Ebenezer led directly by Old Fort, while the opening of two roads would bring both those towns within a four hour's ride of the settlement.

Well content, therefore, with their new acquisition, the Moravians returned to Fort Argyle, whence Johnson rode back to Savannah, leaving them to follow with the boat. At the mouth of the Ogeechee they encountered a severe storm, against which they could make little headway, try as they would. Their anchor was too light to hold against the current, and there was a marsh on one bank and rocks on the other, but at last, after night-fall, in the face of a terrific thunder storm, they forced their way to a place where they could land, and where they passed the rest of the night, enduring as best they could the heavy rain, and the attack of insects, against neither of which they were able to protect themselves. "This place takes its name,—'Rotten-possum,'—from an animal frequently found here, which they call a Possum. I am told that it has a double belly, and that if pursued it puts its young into one belly, runs up a tree until it reaches a limb, springs out on that until it is among the leaves, and then lays itself across the branch with one belly on each side, and so hides itself, and saves its life!" The rest of the journey was uneventful, and on Friday morning, September 2nd, they reached Savannah, having been absent ten days.

It seems a great pity that the Moravians were unable to establish themselves on this tract, where their industry would soon have made an oasis in the wilderness, but one thing after the other interfered, and the " second company " which arrived early in the following year, found them still at Savannah.

In Savannah matters moved toward a fair degree of prosperity for the Moravians. About four acres of Spangenberg's garden were cleared in time for the first summer's crop of corn, which yielded them sixty bushels. They also raised some beans, which came to maturity at a time when provisions and funds were very low, so helping them greatly.

The two farm lots were laid out during the summer, Spangenberg assisting with the survey. By the close of the year twenty-six acres had been cleared,—on the uplands this meant the felling of trees, and gradual removal of stumps as time permitted, but on the rice lands it meant far more. The great reeds, ten to twelve feet high, grew so thick that a man could scarcely set foot between them, and in cutting them down it was necessary to go " knee-deep " below the surface of the ground, and then the roots were so intertwined that it was difficult to pull them out.

Every acre of land that was cleared and planted had to be securely fenced in, for cattle roamed in the woods, and ruined unprotected crops. Indeed, the colonists in Georgia derived little benefit from their cattle, which ran at large, and when a few were wanted for beef or for domestic purposes, they were hunted and driven in. The Moravians had to wait until midsummer before they could get their allotment, and then they received a cow and calf, six hogs and five pigs, with the promise of more. Before the others came the cows had again escaped to the woods, and the swine had been drowned!

In July Spangenberg wrote to Herrnhut that he had given his fifty acres of land, including the town-lot, to the Moravian Congregation at Savannah, and that he would at once apply to the Trustees to vest the title in that body, and if he left Georgia before this was accomplished he would give a full Power of Attorney to Töltschig. From the first his land had been used as the common property of the party, and he desired that the nine men, who, with him, were bound to the repayment of the £60, borrowed from the Trustees, should have the use of it until that obligation was met, and then it should be used as the Savannah Congregation thought best.

Nitschmann's land seems to have been held in a different way, although granted at the same time, and under similar circumstances. July 11th, Spangenberg sent him a detailed description of the town and garden lots, explaining the advantages and difficulties of cultivation, suggesting several methods by which it could be done, and giving the approximate cost, urging that instructions be sent as to his wishes. Later he wrote that the company had decided not to wait for Nitschmann's reply, but to clear the garden on the terms usual in Georgia, *i. g.*, that the man who cleared a piece of ground held it rent free for seven years, when it reverted to the owner. This had been done, and the garden was ready to plant and fence, and if Nitschmann approved they intended to clear the farm, and would build a small house on the town lot. Zinzendorf had suggested that negroes be employed on Nitschmann's land, but at that time slavery was prohibited in Georgia, and any negroes who ran away from Carolina were at once returned to their masters.

The two farms lay side by side about four miles from Savannah, the gardens, also adjoining, were about two miles from town, so it was necessary to build cabins at both places, as shelters from sun and storm, which the settlers found equally trying. Two additional cabins had been built in Savannah on Spangenberg's lot, and by the end of the year a house, thirty-four by eighteen feet in size, was under roof, though not yet finished. This gave an abundance of room, not only for themselves, but for the second company to whose arrival they were looking forward with such eagerness.

When this reinforcement came they hoped to move to Zinzendorf's tract, and then, as soon as they could be spared, Demuth, Haberecht, Waschke and the two Haberlands wished to claim the twenty acres apiece which the Trustees had promised to the Count's "servants." Riedel was of the same mind, but he did not live to see the arrival of the second company. Some months after reaching Georgia, he was dangerously ill with fever, but passed the crisis successfully, and recovered his full strength. He was one of the party who went to survey Zinzendorf's tract, but was taken sick again three days after the boat left Savannah, and by the time they returned he was obliged to go to bed, and soon became delirious. The other Moravians were greatly distressed, but could do nothing except nurse him carefully and pray for him earnestly, and toward the end his mind cleared, though his body had lost the power to recuperate. He died on the 30th of September, the first Moravian to "fall asleep" in the United States, though others had given up their lives for the mission work in the West Indies. His spiritual condition had at times caused much concern to Töltschig, who was especially charged with the religious welfare of the first company, many of whom had been under his care in Germany, but in the main he had been an earnest man, a willing and industrious partaker in the common toil, and his death caused much regret. The burial customs in Savannah included the ringing of bells, a funeral sermon, and a volley of musketry, but learning that these ceremonies were not obligatory the Moravians declined the offer of the citizens to so honor their Brother, and laid him to rest in the Savannah cemetery with a simple service of hymns and prayer.

As they were robing Riedel for his burial, a young man came to the door, and asked if he could not make them some pewter spoons. In the conversations that followed it developed that he was a native of Switzerland, the son of a physician, and after his father's death he had sailed for Pennsylvania, intending there to begin the practice of medicine. But his fellow-passengers stole his books and everything he had, he was unable to pay for his transportation, and forced to sell his service for seven years as a redemptioner. At the end of five years he had become quite ill, and his master, having waited six months for his recovery, heartlessly turned him out, to live or die as the case might be. Instead of dying, his strength returned, and then his former master demanded £10: Pennsylvania currency, for his

The First Year in Georgia. 81

unexpired term, although only £5 : had been paid for him, and he had served five years. The young man was obliged to promise to pay this, and Spangenberg encouraged him to push his spoon-making, in order to do it as speedily as possible. Meanwhile the Moravians were so much pleased with his appearance and speech, that they agreed to receive him into their company for as long as he chose to stay, and John Regnier soon became an important factor in their comfort. Spiritually he was somewhat at sea. At one time he had desired to be a hermit, and then he had drifted from one sect to another, seeking something which he could not find, but acquiring a medley of odd customs. Spangenberg advised him to turn his thoughts from men to God, learning from Him "what was better and higher, Faith, Love, Hope, etc.," and under the Moravian influence he gradually laid aside his unwise fancies, giving them encouragement to believe that he would eventually come into the clearer light, as they knew it.

In material things John Regnier was of great assistance, owing to his ability to turn his hand to almost anything. The shoes of the party were badly torn, but though they had brought leather and tools from England none of them knew the cobbler's trade. John Regnier had never made a shoe, but he took it up, and soon provided for them all, and then he mended their clothing, and added new garments. He also showed much aptitude for nursing, and Spangenberg put him in charge of several cases. A man from a neighboring village sent word that he had severed an artery and could not check the bleeding, and asked for help. Regnier went to him, and was so successful in his treatment that in two weeks the man was entirely restored. Some one discovered a poor Scotchman, dying with dropsy, lying utterly neglected upon the floor of a miserable hut, and appeal was made to the Moravians to take him and care for him. They did so, moving him to one of their cabins, where they made him a bed, and Regnier nursed him until death ended his sufferings. Another man had high fever, and no friends, and him also the Moravians took, and cared for, the Trustee's agent furnishing food and medicine for the sick, but offering no recompense for the care they received.

Indeed, as the months passed by, the Moravians established a reputation for charity and for hospitality. Not only had they kept free of dispute with the Salzburgers, but the friendliest relations existed, and the Moravian cabins were always open to them when they came to Savannah. Nor were they slow to avail themselves of the kindness. Gronau and Bolzius often lodged with them, and others came in groups of nine or ten to spend the night. During the evening stories would be exchanged as to their circumstances in the home lands, and their reasons for leaving there, and then sometimes the hosts would spread hay upon the floor for their guests, at other times give up their own beds, and themselves sleep upon the floor.

With their nearer neighbors in Savannah, they were also upon cordial terms, though they found few who cared for religious things. The Jews were particularly courteous to them, inviting Spangenberg into their Synagogue, and bringing gifts of meat and fish on several occasions when help was sorely needed on account of the illness of some of their number,—for Riedel was not the only one who was seriously ill, though no others died. All the conditions in Georgia were so different from what they were accustomed to in Germany that it took them some time to adapt themselves, and longer to become really acclimated, and they noticed that the same was true of all new-comers. All of the Moravians were sick in turn, many suffering from frosted feet, probably injured on the voyage over, but Spangenberg, Töltschig, Haberecht and Demuth were dangerously ill. Nearly all of the medicine brought from Europe was gone, and what they could get in Savannah was expensive and they did not understand how to use it, so they were forced to depend on careful nursing and simple remedies. Turpentine could easily be secured from the pines, Spangenberg found an herb which he took to be camomile, which had a satisfactory effect, and with the coming of the cooler autumn weather most of the party recovered their health.

Probably the food was partly responsible for their troubles, though they tried to be careful, and cooked everything thoroughly. Rice and salt-meat were their chief articles of diet, for bread cost so much that they soon gave it up entirely, substituting cornmeal mush, and butter was so dear as to be entirely out of the question. During the summer months which preceded the harvest, they could get neither corn, rice nor beans at the store, so lived on mush, salt-meat, and the beans they themselves had planted. Fresh meat was a great treat, particularly when it enabled them to prepare nourishing broth for their sick, and once Rose shot a stag, giving them several good meals, but this happened so seldom as to do little toward varying the monotony of their fare.

Drinking water was held to be responsible for the swollen feet and nausea from which many of them suffered, so they made a kind of sassafras beer, which proved palatable and healthful, and used it until they had become accustomed to the climate, when they were able to drink the water.

When the Moravians came to Georgia they brought with them a little ready money, the gift of English friends, and their cash payments secured them good credit at the Trustees' store. Other merchants sought their patronage, but they decided to run an account at one place only, and thought Mr. Causton, as the Trustees' agent, would give them the most liberal treatment. Their hardest time financially, as well as regarding health, was during the summer, when credit came to be accorded grudgingly, and finally Spangenberg, personally, borrowed £15: sterling, and applied it on their account, which restored their standing in Mr. Causton's eyes. On Feb. 8th, 1736, they decided to buy enough corn, rice and salt-meat to last until harvest, having learned by sad experience how very dear these necessities were later in the year. Very little work had been done which brought in ready money, for their time had been fully occupied in building their house and clearing the land, but all things were prepared for the coming of the second company, with whose assistance they expected to accomplish much. In February the two carpenters were engaged to build a house for Mr. Wagner, a Swiss gentleman who had recently arrived, and rented one of the Moravian cabins temporarily, and this was the beginning of a considerable degree of activity.

The intercourse of the Moravians with the other residents of Savannah was much impeded by their ignorance of the English language, and it occurred to Spangenberg that it might be a good thing to take an English boy, have him bound to them according to custom, and let them learn English by having to speak to him. About July a case came to his knowledge that roused all his sympathies, and at the same time afforded a good opportunity to try his plan. "I have taken a four-year-old English boy into our family. He was born in Charlestown, but somehow found his way to Savannah. His father was hanged, for murder I have heard, and his mother has married another man, and abandoned the child. A woman here took charge of him, but treated him most cruelly. Once she became angry with him, took a firebrand, and beat him until half his body was burned; another time she bound him, and then slashed him with a knife across the back, and might have injured him still more if a man had not come by and rescued him. The magistrates then gave him to other people, but they did not take care of him, and hearing that he was a bright child, I decided to offer to take him. The Magistrates gladly agreed, and will write to his relatives in Charlestown, and if they do not claim him he will be bound to us. He is already proving useful to the Brethren, as he speaks English to them, and they are rapidly learning to speak and to understand. I am sending him to an English school, as I would rather he would not learn German, but being bright he is learning a good deal of it from the Brethren."

On October 31st a widow and her seven-year-old son were received into their household. The woman was in destitute circumstances, and anxious to work, so after four weeks' trial she was installed as maid, and promised $14.00 a year wages. She proved to be quiet and industrious, but not very bright. On Dec. 17th another boy, six years old, was taken, his mother being dead, and his father a day-laborer who could not care for him.

Of the Indians the Moravians had seen a good deal, but no start had been made toward teaching them, except that some of their words had been learned. Spangenberg decided that the only way to master their language would be to go and live among them, and this Rose professed himself willing to do as soon as he could be spared. With Tomochichi they were much pleased. "He is a grave, wise man, resembling one of the old Philosophers, though with him it is natural, not acquired. Were he among a hundred Indians, all clothed alike, one would point him out and say, 'that is the king.'" When the Indians came to the Moravian cabins they were courteously received, and supplied with food and drink, often remaining as silent listeners at the evening service. In turn their good will took the form of a gift of grouse or dried venison, which the Moravians gratefully received.

The English were very anxious to keep the friendship of these Indians, on whom much of their safety depended, and when one of the nations came five or six hundred miles to renew a treaty with

The First Year in Georgia. 87

them, they planned a spectacle which would at once please and impress them. All the settlers were put under arms, and led out to meet them, saluting them with a volley of musketry. With great pomp they were conducted into the town, presented with guns, clothing, etc., and then, through an interpreter, they were assured of the good will and faith of the English, and urged to be true to the treaty, and protect the settlement against those Indian tribes who were under French and Spanish influence.

Spangenberg was ordered out with the others, but excused himself on the ground of weakness from his recent illness, and when the officials offered to depart from their custom, and allow one of Zinzendorf's "servants" to take his place, he explained that the Moravians did not understand English, and knew nothing of military manoeuvres. During the first year the question of military service was not sufficiently prominent to cause real uneasiness, but Spangenberg foresaw trouble, and wrote to Herrnhut, urging that the matter be given serious consideration.

When the Moravians passed through London they had fully explained their position to Gen. Oglethorpe, who promised them exemption, but they had no written order from the Trustees to show to the local officials, and not even a copy of the letter in which reference to the subject was made. As Count Zinzendorf's "servants" nine of them were ineligible, but Spangenberg, as a free-holder, was expected to take part in the weekly drill, which he quietly refused to do.

All free-holders were likewise expected to take

their turn in the Watch, composed of ten men, who patrolled the town by night and day. Spangenberg admitted that the Watch was necessary and proper, but decided that he had better not take a personal share in it, other than by hiring some one to take his place, which was permitted. As the turn came every seventeen days, and a man expected fifty cents for day and one dollar for night duty each time, this was expensive, doubly so because the officers demanded a substitute for the absent Nitschmann also. Twice had Spangenberg been before the Court, attempting to have the matter adjusted, but he found that this, like many other things, could not be settled until Gen. Oglethorpe came. "All men wait for Gen. Oglethorpe, it is impossible to describe how they long for him." The Salzburgers especially wished for him, for they did not like the place where they had settled, and wanted permission to move to a more favorable location which they had chosen.

On the 14th of February, 1736, Capt. Thomson arrived, bringing letters from England, and one to Spangenberg announced that the second company of Moravians was on the way and might soon be expected. At three o'clock in the morning of February 17th, the town was roused by the sound of bells and drums. Thinking it meant fire, the Moravians rushed out, but learned that Gen. Oglethorpe's ship had reached Tybee, and the people were awakened to welcome him. Full of interest to learn whether the second company was with him the Moravians paused for a hasty meal before going to meet the ship, when to their great joy Bishop Nitschmann appeared before them, "and his face was to us as the face of an Angel!"

Chapter IV.

REINFORCEMENTS.

the "second company."

Before David Nitschmann, the "Hausmeister," left London, after the sailing of the first Moravian company for Georgia, he presented to the Trustees a series of propositions, the acceptance of which would open the way for a large increase of Moravian emigration. The proposals were, in brief, that the Trustees should give credit to the Moravians to the extent of £500 sterling, which, deducting the £60 advanced to the first company, would provide passage money and a year's provision for fifty-five more of Count Zinzendorf's "servants," the loan to be repaid, without interest, in five years, and to bear interest at the usual rate if payment was longer deferred. He also suggested that the money, when repaid, should be again advanced for a like purpose.

In addition he requested that each man of twenty-one years, or over, should be granted fifty acres near Count Zinzendorf's tract.

The Trustees were pleased to approve of these proposals, and promised the desired credit, with the further favor that if the debt was not paid within five years it should draw interest at eight per cent. only, instead of ten per cent., the customary rate in South Carolina.

During the summer, therefore, a second company prepared to follow the pioneers to the New World.

On the 5th of August, 1735, two parties left Herrnhut, one consisting of three young men, and the other of thirteen men, women and children, who were joined at Leipzig by Jonas Korte, who went with them to London. On August 8th, five more persons left Herrnhut, under the leadership of David Nitschmann, the Bishop, who was to take the second company to Georgia, organize their congregation, and ordain their pastor.

This David Nitschmann, a carpenter by trade, was a companion of David Nitschmann, the "Hausmeister," and John Töltschig, when they left Moravia in the hope of re-establishing the Unitas Fratrum, and with them settled at Herrnhut, and became one of the influential members of the community. When missionaries were to be sent to the Danish West Indies, Nitschmann and Leonard Dober went on foot to Copenhagen (August 21st, 1732), and sailed from there, Nitschmann paying their way by his work as ship's carpenter. By the same handicraft he supported himself and his companion for four months on the island of St. Thomas, where they preached to the negro slaves, and then, according to previous arrangement, he left Dober to continue the work, and returned to Germany. In 1735, it was decided that Bishop Jablonski, of Berlin, and Bishop Sitkovius, of Poland, who represented the Episcopate of the ancient Unitas Fratrum, should consecrate one of the members of the renewed Unitas Fratrum at Herrnhut, linking the Church of the Fathers with that of their descendents, and enabling the latter to send to the Mission field ministers whose ordination could not be questioned by other denominations, or by the civil authorities.

David Nitschmann, then one of the Elders at Herrnhut, was chosen to receive consecration, the service being performed, March 13th, by Bishop Jablonski, with the written concurrence of Bishop Sitkovius.

The three parties from Herrnhut met at Magdeburg on August 13th, proceeding from there to Hamburg by boat, and at Altona, the sea-port of Hamburg, they found ten more colonists who had preceded them. Here also they were joined by Christian Adolph von Hermsdorf, who went with them to Georgia as "a volunteer." Apparently Lieutenant Hermsdorf wanted the position of Zinzendorf's Agent in Georgia, for the Count wrote to him on the 19th of August, agreeing that he should go with the Moravians, at their expense, but saying that if he desired office he must first prove himself worthy of it by service with and for the others, even as the Count had always done. If the reports from Georgia justified it, the Count promised to send him proper powers later, and to find a good opportunity for his wife to follow him. Rosina Schwarz and her child, who had come with them to Hamburg to meet her husband, returned with him to their home in Holstein; and on account of Rosina Neubert's serious illness, she and her husband reluctantly agreed to leave the company, and wait for another opportunity to go to Georgia. In 1742 they carried out their intention of emigrating to America, though it was to Pennsylvania, and not to Georgia.

The "second company," therefore, consisted of twenty-five persons:

David Nitschmann, the Bishop.
Christian Adolph von Hermsdorf, a volunteer.

John Andrew Dober, a potter.
David Zeisberger.
David Tanneberger, a shoemaker.
John Tanneberger, son of David, a boy of ten years.
George Neisser.
Augustin Neisser, a young lad, brother of George.
Henry Roscher, a linen-weaver.
David Jag.
John Michael Meyer, a tailor.
Jacob Frank.
John Martin Mack.
Matthias Seybold, a farmer.
Gottlieb Demuth.
John Böhner, a carpenter.
Matthias Böhnish.
Maria Catherine Dober, wife of John Andrew Dober.
Rosina Zeisberger, wife of David Zeisberger.
Judith Töltschig, Catherine Riedel, Rosina Haberecht, Regina Demuth, going to join their husbands already in Georgia.
Anna Waschke, a widow, to join her son.
Juliana Jäschke, a seamstress.*

During an enforced stay of three weeks at Altona, the Moravians experienced much kindness, especially at the hands of Korte and his family, and Mrs. Weintraube, the daughter of a Mennonite preacher, who had come from her home in London on a visit to her father. By this time the Moravian settlement at Herrnhut was coming to be well and

---

*Fifteen of these colonists were originally from Moravia and Bohemia.

favorably known in Holland, and every visit won new friends, many of whom came into organic fellowship with them. A few years later, when the Unitas Fratrum was confronted by a great financial crisis, it was largely the loyalty and liberality of the Dutch members that enabled it to reach a position of safety.

On the 9th of September, the company went aboard an English boat, homeward bound, but contrary winds held them in port until the 13th, and it was not until Sunday, Oct. 2nd, that they reached London, after a long and stormy crossing, which gave many of them their first experience of sea-sickness.

Nitschmann and Korte at once went ashore to report their arrival to Secretary Verelst, and on Monday a house was rented, and the twenty-five colonists and Jonas Korte moved into it, to wait for the sailing of Gen Oglethorpe's ship, the General having offered them berths on his own vessel. The General was out of town when they reached London, but called on Monday evening, and showed them every kindness,—"Oglethorpe is indeed our good friend, and cares for us like a father."

Nitschmann found a good deal of difficulty on account of the language, for he could not speak Latin, as Spangenberg had done, and knew no English, so that all of his conversations with Oglethorpe had to be carried on through an interpreter; nevertheless a number of important points were fully discussed.

On the question of military service he could reach no definite and satisfactory conclusion, and thought it a great pity that there had not been a perfect mutual understanding between Zinzendorf and the Trustees before the first company sailed. That Zinzendorf's "servants" should be free from military service was admitted by all, but Oglethorpe thought three men must be furnished to represent Zinzendorf, Spangenberg and Nitschmann (the Hausmeister), the three free-holders, and suggested that Lieutenant Hermsdorf might take one place. Nitschmann said that would not do, that the Moravians "could not and would not fight," and there the matter rested. Nitschmann wrote to Zinzendorf, begging him to come to London, and interview the Trustees, but advised that he wait for Oglethorpe's return from Georgia some nine months later.

On this account the members of the second company agreed that it would be better for them not to accept land individually, but to go, as the others had done, as Zinzendorf's "servants," to work on his tract. Oglethorpe suggested that an additional five hundred acres should be requested for Count Zinzendorf's son, and Nitschmann referred the proposal to the authorities at Herrnhut. In regard to the five hundred acre tract already granted, the General said that it had been located near the Indians, at the Moravians' request, but that settlers there would be in no danger, for the Indians were at peace with the English, there was a fort near by, and besides he intended to place a colony of Salzburgers fifty miles further south, when the Moravians would be, not on the border but in the center of Georgia.

Gen. Oglethorpe assured Nitschmann that there

would be no trouble regarding the transfer of title to the Georgia lands, for while, for weighty reasons, the grants had been made in tail male, there was no intention, on the part of the Trustees, to use this as a pretext for regaining the land, and if there was no male heir, a brother, or failing this, a friend, might take the title. (In 1739 the law entailing property in Georgia was modified to meet this view, and after 1750, all grants were made in fee simple.) He also explained that the obligation to plant a certain number of mulberry trees per acre, or forfeit the land, was intended to spur lazy colonists, and would not be enforced in the case of the Moravians.

Nitschmann told Gen. Oglethorpe of the wives and children who had been left in Herrnhut, and suggested the advisability of establishing an English School for them, that they might be better fitted for life in Georgia. Oglethorpe liked the idea, and, after due consideration, suggested that some one in Herrnhut who spoke French or Latin, preferably the latter, should be named as Count Zinzendorf's Agent, to handle funds for the English school, and to accompany later companies of Georgia colonists as far as London, his expenses to be paid by the Trustees. Of this the Trustees approved, and donated £40 sterling, partly for Nitschmann's use in London, and the balance,—about £4 it proved to be,—for the Herrnhut school. An English gentleman also gave them £32, with the proviso that within four years they in turn would give an equal amount to the needy, which Nitschmann readily agreed should be done.

Various other gifts must have been received, for

when the company sailed, Nitschmann reported to Count Zinzendorf that, without counting a considerable amount which Korte had generously expended on their behalf, they had received £115 in London, and had spent £113. "This will seem much to you, but when you look over the accounts, and consider the number of people, and how dear everything is, you will understand." Unfortunately the colonists had left Herrnhut without a sufficient quantity of warm clothing, thinking that it would not be needed, but letters from Georgia gave them quite new ideas of the climate there, and they were forced to supply themselves in London, though at double what it would have cost in Germany.

In addition to these expenditures, the second company borrowed from the Trustees the funds for their passage to Georgia, and a year's provision there, binding themselves jointly and severally to repay the money, the bond, dated Oct. 26th, 1735, being for the sum of £453 : 7 : 6 :, double the amount of the actual debt. This included

Passage for 16 men, 8 women and 1 boy, 25 persons, 24½ "heads"......	£122 : 10 : 0
25 sets of bed-clothes...............	6 : 5 : 0
1 year's provisions in Georgia, being 12 bushels Indian Corn, 100 lbs. Meat, 30 lbs. Butter, 1 bushel Salt, 27 lbs. Cheese, per head...........	64 : 6 : 3
Advanced in London for necessaries...	33 : 12 : 6
	£226 : 13 : 9

This was to be repaid in five years, drawing eight per cent. interest after three years, further security to be given within twelve months if requested by the Trustees or their Agent; and any provisions not used to be credited on their account.

In the matter of forming new acquaintances in London, the second company was far less active than the first had been, Spangenberg's standing and education having given him access to many people, attracting their attention to his companions. The second company profited by the friends he had made, Mr. Wynantz especially devoting himself to their service, and while Nitschmann and his associates did not reach many new people, they inspired the respect and confidence of those whom Spangenberg had introduced to the Moravian Church, and so strengthened its cause. A carpenter from Wittenberg, Vollmar by name, who was attracted to them, requested permission to go to Georgia with them, although not at their expense, and to this they agreed. A number of Salzburgers who were to go to Georgia with General Oglethorpe, though not on the same ship, were under the leadership of the young Baron von Reck with whom Zinzendorf had corresponded during the early stages of the Moravian negotiations, and the Baron called on the second company several times, offered to assist them in any way in his power, and expressed the wish that the Moravians and Salzburgers could live together in Georgia. Nitschmann doubted the wisdom of the plan, but courteously agreed to refer it to Zinzendorf, who, however, refused his sanction.

On the 12th of October, the Moravians went aboard Gen. Oglethorpe's ship, the *Simmonds*, Capt. Cornish, where they were told to select the cabins they preferred, being given preference over the English colonists who were going. The cabins contained bare bunks, which could be closed when not in use, arranged in groups of five,—three below and two above,—the five persons occupying them also eating together. The Moravions chose their places in the center of the ship, on either side of the main mast, where the ventilation was best, and there would be most fresh air when they reached warmer latitudes. "The number of people on the ship is rather large, for we are altogether one hundred and fifty who are going to Georgia, but besides ourselves they are all Englishmen." "Many of them are like wild animals, but we have resolved in all things to act as the children of God, giving offence to no one, that our purpose be not misconstrued."

After seeing his companions comfortably settled on the vessel, Nitschmann returned to his numerous tasks in London. On the 24th, he came back to the ship, accompanied by Korte, who bade them an affectionate farewell. By the 27th all of the passengers, including Gen. Oglethorpe, were on board, but it was not until the afternoon of October 31st, that the *Simmonds* sailed from Gravesend.

FOUR JOURNALS.

On the *Simmonds,* as she sailed slowly down the Thames on her way to Georgia, there were four Englishmen, with whom the Moravians were to become well acquainted, who were to influence and be influenced by them, and through whom a great change was to come into the religious history of England. These were John and Charles Wesley,

Benjamin Ingham and Charles Delamotte. The Wesleys were sons of Samuel Wesley, a clergyman of the Church of England, and while at the University of Oxford they, with two companions, had formed a little society for religious improvement, and by their strict and methodical habits gained the name of "Methodists"; both brothers had taken orders in the English Church, and were on their way to Georgia, John to serve as rector at Savannah, and Charles as Gen. Oglethorpe's private secretary. Benjamin Ingham was born in Yorkshire, and met the Wesleys at Oxford, where he joined their Methodist society. He, too, had been ordained in the English Church, and now, at the age of twenty-three, had yielded to John Wesley's persuasions, and agreed to go with him "to the Indians." Charles Delamotte, the son of a London merchant, met the Wesleys at the home of James Hutton, shortly before they sailed for Georgia, and was so much impressed by them, and by their object in seeking the New World, that he decided "to leave the world, and give himself up entirely to God," and go with them.

For the greater part of his life John Wesley kept a Journal, extracts from which were given to the public from time to time, and Benjamin Ingham's account of the voyage to Georgia was also printed, so that the story of those weeks is quite well known. Nevertheless, something of interest may be gained by comparing these two Journals with the Diaries kept by David Nitschmann, Bishop of the Moravians, and John Andrew Dober, one of the second company.

To avoid confusion it should be noted that the difference of eleven days in the dates is only apparent, not real, for the Englishmen used the old style calendar, the Germans employed the modern one. In 46 B. C. the Roman Calendar had gained two months on the actual seasons, and a more accurate calculation resulted in the adoption of the so-called "Julian Calendar" (prepared at the request of Julius Caesar), the two missing months being inserted between November and December in that "year of confusion." By 1582, however, the Julian Calendar had fallen ten days behind the seasons, so another calculation was made, and Pope Gregory XIII. abolished the Julian Calendar in all Catholic countries, dropped the dates of ten days from that year, and established the "reformed," or "Gregorian Calendar." This was adopted in Catholic Germany, in 1583, in Protestant Germany and Holland, in 1700, but in England not until 1752, by which time the difference had increased to eleven days. Following the ancient Jewish custom the Year, for many centuries, began with the 25th of March, but public sentiment came to favor the 1st of January as the more appropriate date, and it was gradually adopted. In England, however, the legal year continued to begin with March 25th, until 1752, although many people were either using the newer fashion, or indicating both, and a date might be correctly written in four ways, *e. g.* January 10th, 1734, old style, legal, January 10th, 1734-5, or January 10th, 1735, old style, popular, and January 21st, 1735, new style, the last agreeing with the calendar now in general use.

Bishop Nitschmann gives the outline of their religious services on almost every day, and in the translation which follows these are generally omitted; in the same way some paragraphs are left out of the Wesley Journal. Extracts from Dober's and Ingham's Journals are inserted when they give facts not otherwise noted.

NITSCHMANN'S DIARY.

Oct. 24th, 1735.—I went to the ship, (the **Simmonds**, Captain Cornish). My heart rejoiced to be once more with the Brethren. In the evening we held our song service.

(We have all given ourselves to the Lord, and pray that the Saviour may comfort our hearts with joy, and that we may attain our object, namely, to call the heathen, to become acquainted with those whom we have not known and who know us not, and to worship the name of the Lord.—Letter of Oct. 28.)

JOHN WESLEY'S JOURNAL.

Oct. 14th, 1735, (O. S.) Tuesday. — Mr. Benjamin Ingham, of Queen's College, Oxford, Mr. Charles Delamotte, son of a merchant in London, who had offered himself some days before, my brother Charles Wesley, and myself, took boat for Gravesend, in order to embark for Georgia. Our end in leaving our native country was not to avoid want, (God having given us plenty of temporal blessings,) nor to gain the dung or dross of riches or honor; but singly this,—to save our souls, to live wholly to the glory of God. In the afternoon we found the **Simmonds** off Gravesend, and immediately went on board.

(We had two cabins allotted us in the forecastle; I and Mr. Delamotte having the first, and Messrs. Wesley the other. Theirs was

Nitschmann's—Continued.

Oct. 27th.—Bled Mrs. Töltschig and Mrs. Zeisberger. On deck one man was knocked down by another, striking his head on the deck so as to stun him. In the evening we held our song service at the same hour that the English had theirs. I spoke with Mr. Oglethorpe and the two English clergymen, who asked concerning our ordination and our faith. Mr. Oglethorpe said he would be as our father, if we would permit it.

Oct. 28th.—At our prayer-meeting considered Eph. 1, how our election may be made sure; I also wrote to the Congregation at Herrnhut. Mrs. Zeisberger was sick, and Mr. Oglethorpe concerned himself about her comfort.

Oct. 29th.—Spoke with the Wittenberg carpenter concerning his soul.

Oct. 30th.—We decided who should attend to vari-

Wesley's—Continued.

made pretty large, so that we could all meet together to read or pray in it. This part of the ship was assigned to us by Mr. Oglethorpe, as being most convenient for privacy.— Ingham's Journal.)

Oct. 17th.—I began to learn German in order to converse with the Germans, six and twenty[*] of whom we had on board.

---

[*] Twenty-five Moravians and the Wittenberg carpenter.

Nitschmann's—Continued.

ous duties during the voyage, and held our "Band" meetings. (The "Bands" were small groups, closely associated for mutual religious improvement.) An English boy fell overboard, but was rescued by a sailor.

Oct. 31st.—In the afternoon we sailed twelve miles from Gravesend.

Nov. 1st.—The English clergyman began to spend an hour teaching us English. In the early service we read concerning new life in the soul; the preceding night was blessed to me, and the Saviour was near. At the evening service we spoke of earnest prayer and its answer. (David Nitschmann, in the presence of all the members, formally installed certain of our members in office,—David Tanne-

Wesley's—Continued.

Oct. 20th, Monday.—Believing the denying ourselves, even in the smallest instances, might, by the blessing of God, be helpful to us, we wholly left off the use of flesh and wine, and confined ourselves to vegetable food,—chiefly rice and biscuit. In the afternoon, David Nitschmann, Bishop of the Germans, and two others, began to learn English. O may we be, not only of one tongue, but of one mind and of one heart.

Oct. 21st.—We sailed from Gravesend. When we were past about half the Goodwin Sands the wind suddenly failed. Had the calm continued till ebb, the ship had probably been lost. But the gale sprung up again in an hour, and carried us into the Downs.

We now began to be a little regular. Our common way of living was this: From four in the morning till five, each of us used pri-

Nitschmann's—Continued.

berger as overseer, Dober as teacher and monitor, Seybold as nurse for the brethren, and Mrs. Dober as nurse for the sisters.—Dober's Diary.)

(We have arranged that one of us shall watch each night, of which Mr. Oglethorpe approves.—Letter of Oct. 18th.)

Nov. 2nd.—We sailed further. In the early prayer service we considered Eph. IV, the unity of the Spirit, and the means of preserving the bond of peace. In the song service many points of doctrine were discussed with the English clergyman, also the decline and loss of power.

Nov. 3rd.—A dense fog and unpleasant weather, so we lay still at anchor.

Wesley's—Continued.

vate prayer. From five to seven we read the Bible together, carefully comparing it (that we might not lean to our own understanding) with the writings of the earliest ages. At seven we breakfasted. At eight were the public prayers. From nine to twelve I usually learned German and Mr. Delamotte Greek. My brother writ sermons, and Mr. Ingham instructed the children. At twelve we met to give an account to one another what we had done since our last meeting, and what we designed to do before our next. About one we dined. The time from dinner to four, we spent in reading to those whom each of us had taken in charge, or in speaking to them severally, as need required. At four were the Evening Prayers; when either the Second Lesson was explained (as it always was in the morning,) or the children were catechised, and instructed before the congregation. From five to six we again used private prayer. From six to seven I read in our cabin to two or three of the passengers, (of whom there were about

Nitschmann's—Continued.

Nov. 4th.—I visited the other ship, (the **London Merchant**, Capt. Thomas) where the so-called Salzburgers are. I spend most of my time studying English.

Nov. 5th.—We prayed for the Congregation at Herrnhut, and also that we might be one with it in spirit. In the evening we spoke of the Lord's protection, how good it is.
There is no room for fear,
The world may shake and quiver,
The elements may rage,
The firmament may shiver,
We are safe-guarded.

Nov. 8th.—An (English) child died, and was buried in the sea at five o'clock.

Wesley's—Continued.

eighty English on board), and each of my brethren to a few more in theirs. At seven I joined with the Germans in their public service; while Mr. Ingham was reading between the decks to as many as desired to hear. At eight we met again, to exhort and instruct one another. Between nine and ten we went to bed, where neither the roaring of the sea, nor the motion of the ship, could take away the refreshing sleep which God gave us.

Oct. 24th.—Having a rolling sea, most of the passengers found the effects of it. Mr. Delamotte was exceeding sick for several days, Mr. Ingham for about half an hour. My brother's head ached much. Hitherto it has pleased God the sea has not disordered me at all.

During our stay in the Downs, some or other of us went, as often as we had opportunity, on board the ship that sailed in company with us, where also many were glad to join in prayer and hearing the word.

Nitschmann's—Continued.

Nov. 11th.—The text was "The Lord is with me, therefore I do not fear."

Nov. 12th.—(This afternoon we came near Portsmouth, and anchored. To-day Dober began to study English, and learned the Lord's Prayer.—Dober's Diary.)

Nov. 13th.—Hermsdorf visits Baron von Reck.

Nov. 14th.—We lay at anchor at Cowes on the Isle of Wight, and some of us landed. I went with Baron von Reck to Newport, one mile distant, it is a beautiful place. I conversed with Baron von Reck about the Lord's Prayer.

Nov. 18th.—A great storm. To me the time is precious, and passes too swiftly. It is as though we were in the midst of wild beasts, which are bound and cannot harm us. We know the Saviour stands by us, and strengthens us through the Holy Ghost.

Wesley's—Continued.

Oct. 31st.—We sailed out of the Downs. At eleven at night I was waked by a great noise. I soon found there was no danger. But the bare apprehension of it gave me a lively conviction what manner of men those ought to be, who are every moment on the brink of eternity.

Nov. 1st, Saturday.—We came to St. Helen's harbour, and the next day into Cowes road. The wind was fair, but we waited for the man-of-war which was to sail with us. This was a happy opportunity of instructing our fellow travellers. May He whose seed we sow, give it the increase!

Nitschmann's—Continued.

Nov 20th.—One older and two young Englishmen were whipped for stealing.

Nov. 21st.—Conversed with Mr. Oglethorpe about our ordination, Baron von Reck acting as interpreter. He was well pleased when I explained our view, and that we did not think a Bishop must be a great lord as among the Catholics. He offered to give us anything we wished, but I told him we needed nothing.

Nov. 23rd.—The Man-of-war (Hawk, Capt. Gascoine) joined us. A boy was beaten, and sent away from the ship.

Nov. 25th.—Spoke with Mr. Oglethorpe about Böhner and George Neisser, who are sick and must go ashore for treatment. Böhner has a sore arm, and Neisser a sore foot. An English friend gave us a guinea to buy some things we need.

Nov. 29th.—In the evening I prayed for a good wind, since we do not wish to lie in one place and be of no use.

Dec. 1st.—The wind was good, we thanked God and sailed about eight o'clock. Not long after the wind fell,

Wesley's—Continued.

Nov. 20th.—We fell down Yarmouth road, but the next day were forced back to Cowes. During our stay

Nitschmann's—Continued.

and we anchored, but I could not believe that we were not to go. The wind rose again, and we sailed nine miles.

Dec. 2nd.—About two o'clock we returned to Cowes.

Dec. 3rd.—The women went ashore to wash our clothes. The others went with them, because we do not wish to annoy any one, and desired to be alone that we might celebrate the Lord's Supper. I could not leave the ship, but was with them in spirit.

Dec. 4th.—(Nitschmann and Dober spoke with several of the Brethren concerning their spiritual condition. In the evening a storm sprang up which continued most of the night. Mr. Oglethorpe is ill, which reminds us to pray for him, and the English preacher, John Wesley, has promised to do the same. This preacher loses no opportunity to be present at our song service; he spares no pains to perform the duties of his office and he likes us. We wish we could converse freely with him, so that we could more carefully explain

Wesley's—Continued.

here there were several storms, in one of which two ships in Yarmouth roads were lost.

The continuance of the contrary winds gave my brother an opportunity of complying with the desire of the minister of Cowes, and preaching there three or four times.

Nov. 23rd, Sunday.—At night I was waked by the tossing of the ship, and roaring of the wind, and plainly showed I was unfit, for I was unwilling to die.

Nitschmann's—Continued.

the way of God to him.—Dober's Diary.)

Dec. 7th.—A great storm, and we thanked God that we were in a safe harbor.

Dec. 10th.—All hands summoned to lift the anchor. Mr. Oglethorpe called me, took me by the hand, led me into the cabin, and gave me £1 for the Brethren. Later the wind was again contrary, and we had to lie still.

Dec. 18th.—We lifted the anchor at three o'clock, but as we got under sail the wind changed again. We must stay still, but what the Lord intends we do not know.

Dec. 21st.—An east wind sprang up, and with the help of God we sailed at nine o'clock from Cowes, where we had been for five weeks and three days. (With us went two ships, the man-of-war, and that which carried Baron von Reck and his Salzburgers. Two of the Salzburgers were on shore, and were left behind when the ship sailed, whereat their wives and children who were on board, were sorely grieved.—Dober's Diary.)

Wesley's—Continued.

Dec. 7th, Sunday.—Finding nature did not require such frequent supplies as we had been accustomed to, we agreed to leave off suppers; from doing which we have hitherto found no inconvenience.

Dec. 10th, Wednesday.—We sailed from Cowes, and in the afternoon passed the Needles. From this day to the fourteenth being in the Bay of Biscay, the sea was very rough. Mr. Delamotte and others were more sick than ever; Mr. Ingham a little; I not at all. But the fourteenth being a calm day, most of the sick were cured at once.

Nitschmann's—Continued.

When we reached the open sea many became sea-sick. There was so much to be done that we could not hold our prayer-meeting, for our people help in all the work, and therefore the sailors treat us well, no matter what they think of us in their hearts. In the evening our song service was much blessed.

Dec. 22nd.—The wind was east, and we sailed nine miles an hour, but were all very sea-sick.

Dec. 25th.—As this was Christmas Day we read Matt. VIII. in our prayer service. The wind had died down, everyone felt much better, and it was a beautiful day.

Dec. 27th.—At midnight there was a great storm, and the waves broke over the ship; the middle hatch was open, and the water poured in, running into our cabin, so that we had to take everything out of them until we could dry them.

Dec. 30th.—The weather was again pleasant.

Wesley's—Continued.

Dec. 12th.—(In the forenoon we left the man-of-war, he not being able to sail as fast as our ships.—Ingham's Journal.)

(Dec. 19th.—Messrs. Wesley and I, with Mr. Oglethorpe's approbation, undertook to visit, each of us, a part of the ship, and daily to provide the sick people

GENERAL JAMES OGLETHORPE.
From a pen sketch in the Herrnhut Archives.

Nitschmann's—Continued.

Jan. 1, 1736.—It was New Year's Day, and Mr. Oglethorpe's birthday. (Br. Nitschmann asked us to select a number of verses, wrote them out and presented them as a birthday greeting to Mr. Oglethorpe. It was a beautiful day, warm and calm.—Dober's Diary.)

Jan. 5th.—(To-day, according to the old style, Christmas was celebrated on our ship. Br. Nitschmann spoke on the words, "Unto us a Child is born, unto us a Son is given."—Dober's Diary.)

Jan. 10th.—(We have been running for several days with the Trade winds. Here the day is two hours longer than it is in Germany at this season. The sailors wished to adhere to their custom of initiating those who crossed the Tropic of Cancer for the first time,

Wesley's—Continued.

with water-gruel, and such other things as were necessary for them.—Ingham's Journal.)

Dec. 21st, Sunday.—We had fifteen communicants, which was our usual number on Sundays.

(This being Mr. Oglethorpe's birthday, he gave a sheep and wine to the people, which, with the smoothness of the sea, and the serenity of the sky, so enlivened them that they perfectly recovered from their sea-sickness.

On Christmas Day, also, Mr Oglethorpe gave a hog and wine to the people.—Ingham's Journal.)

Dec. 29th.—(We are now past the latitude of twenty-five degrees, and are got into what they call the Trade winds, which blow much the same way all the year round. The air is balmy, soft, and sweet. The ship glides smoothly and quietly along. The

Nitschmann's—Continued.

but Gen. Oglethorpe forbade it. The weak, the children, and the sick, are well cared for, so that the nine months' old child receives an egg and some goat's milk every day.—Dober's Diary.)

Jan. 12th.—To-day, according to the old style, we celebrated the New Year.

Jan. 20th.—An English clergyman asked us how often we celebrated the Lord's Supper, saying that he thought it a sacrifice which consecrated and improved the life. We told him our view; he said he would like to visit Herrnhut.

(We re-crossed the Tropic of Cancer.—Dober's Diary.)

Jan. 21st.—(We are still in the Trade wind, and sail swiftly and steadily.) We cannot thank God enough that we are all well, only Mrs. Demuth is always seasick when the wind rises.

Jan. 23rd.—We saw a ship.

Jan. 27th.—(As there was little good water left the passengers were given poor water, but when Oglethorpe

Wesley's—Continued.

nights are mild and pleasant, being beautifully adorned with the shining hosts of stars,

"Forever singing as they shine,
The Hand that made us is divine."
—Ingham's Journal.)

Jan. 12th, 1736.—(I began to write out the English Dictionary in order to learn the Indian tongue.- Ingham's Journal.)

Jan. 15th.—Complaint being made to Mr. Oglethorpe of the unequal distribution of the water among the pas-

Nitschmann's—Continued.

heard of it, he ordered that all, in the Cabin and outside, should be treated alike, as long as the good water lasted. Mr. Oglethorpe and the preacher, John Wesley, are very careful of the passengers' welfare; the latter shows himself full of love for us.—Dober's Diary.)

Jan. 28th.—There was a great storm, the waves went over the ship, and poured into it. Then many who knew not God were frightened, but we were of good cheer, and trusted in the Lord who does all things well. Roscher and Mack are good sailors and not afraid of anything.

Wesley's—Continued.

sengers, he appointed new officers to take charge of it. At this the old ones and their friends were highly exasperated against us, to whom they imputed the change. But "the fierceness of man shall turn to thy praise."

Jan. 17th, Saturday.—Many people were very impatient at the contrary wind. At seven in the evening they were quieted by a storm. It rose higher and higher till nine. About nine the sea broke over us from stem to stern; burst through the windows of the state cabin, where three or four of us were, and covered us all over, though a bureau sheltered me from the main shock. About eleven I lay down in the great cabin, and in a short time fell asleep, though very uncertain whether I should wake alive, and much ashamed of my unwillingness to die. O how pure in heart must he be, who would rejoice to appear before God at a moment's warning! Toward morning "He rebuked the wind and the sea, and there was a great calm."

Nitschmann's—Continued.

Jan. 29th.—We read the 13th chapter of Mark at our early prayer service. The weather was a little better, but the wind was contrary. We also saw a ship which was sailing northeast. In the evening we read the ninety-eighth Psalm, the Lord was with us and we were blessed.

Feb. 1st.—The weather was fine, and there was no wind until ten o'clock, when it came from the right quarter. In addition to our usual allowance the Captain sent us fresh meat, which he has done thrice already, and we do not altogether like it, for we are content with what we have, and do not desire more.

Feb. 3rd.—There was a great storm, which lasted all night.

Feb. 4th.—The storm lasted all day, and the waves often swept over the ship. The storm rudder was lashed fast, and so we were driven.

Wesley's—Continued.

Jan. 18th, Sunday.—We returned thanks to God for our deliverance, of which a few appeared duly sensible. But the rest (among whom were most of the sailors) denied we had been in any danger. I could not have believed that so little good would have been done by the terror they were in before. But it cannot be that they should long obey God from fear, who are deaf to the motives of love.

Jan. 23rd, Friday.—In the evening another storm began. In the morning it increased, so that they were forced to let the ship drive. I could not but say to myself, "How is it that thou hast no faith?" being still unwilling to die. About one in the afternoon, almost as soon as I had stepped out of the great cabin door, the sea did not break as usual, but came with a smooth full tide over the side of the ship. I was vaulted

Nitschmann's—Continued.

Feb. 5th.—In the early morning we had a fairly good breeze, but about ten o'clock, a storm rose, of such violence that the wind seemed to blow from all four quarters at once, and we were in danger of being overpowered. The waves were like mountains; the rudder was lashed fast, only one sail was spread, and we drove on, only the Lord knew whither. But we did not let it prevent us from holding our song service. The text given to us was Psalm CXV. 14, which assured us that we were blessed of God,—may He ever bless us more and more. During the service the ship was covered with a great wave, which poured in upon us, and on the deck there was a great cry that the wind had split the one sail which was spread. There was great fright among the people who have

Wesley's—Continued.

over with water in a moment, and so stunned, that I scarce expected to lift up my head again, till the sea should give up her dead. But thanks be to God, I received no hurt at all. About noon our third storm began.

Jan. 25th, Sunday.—At noon our third storm began. At four it was more violent than before. The winds roared round about us, and whistled as distinctly as if it had been a human voice. The ship not only rocked to and fro with the utmost violence, but shook and jarred with so unequal, grating, a motion, that one could not but with great difficulty keep one's hold of anything, nor stand a moment without it. Every ten minutes came a shock against the stern or side of the ship, which one would think should dash the planks to pieces.

We spent two or three hours after prayers, in conversing suitably to the occasion, confirming one another in a calm submission to the wise, holy, gracious will of God. And now a storm did not appear so terrible as before. Blessed

Nitschmann's—Continued.

no God; the English clergyman was much aroused, ran to them, and preached repentance, saying among other things that they could now see the difference. I was content, for our lives are in God's hands, and He does what He will; among us there was no fear, for the Lord helped us. (There was a terrible storm which lasted till midnight. During the song service a great wave struck the ship with a noise like the roar of a cannon. The wind tore the strong new sail in two; the people, especially the English women, screamed and wept; the preacher Wesley, who is always with us in our song service, cried out against the English, "Now man can see who has a God, and who has none." During the last eight days we have had so much contrary wind, and so many storms that we could not approach the land, though we were near it several times.—Dober's Diary.)

Wesley's—Continued.

be the God of all consolation!

At seven I went to the Germans; I had long before observed the great seriousness of their behaviour. Of their humility they had given a continual proof, by performing those servile offices for the other passengers, which none of the English would undertake; for which they desired, and would receive no pay, saying "It was good for their proud hearts," and "their loving Saviour had done more for them." And every day had given them occasion of showing a meekness, which no injury could move. If they were pushed, struck, or thrown down, they rose again and went away; but no complaint was found in their mouth. There was now an opportunity of trying whether they were delivered from the spirit of fear, as well as from that of pride, anger, and revenge. In the midst of the psalm wherewith their service began, the sea broke over, split the mainsail in pieces, covered the ship, and poured in between the

Nitschmann's—Continued.	Wesley's—Continued.
	decks, as if the great deep had already swallowed us up. A terrible screaming began among the English. The Germans calmly sung on. I asked one of them afterward, "Was you not afraid?" He answered, "I thank God, no." I asked, "But were not your women and children afraid?" He replied mildly, "No; our women and children are not afraid to die."
	From them I went to their crying, trembling neighbors, and pointed out to them the difference in the hour of trial, between him that feareth God, and him that feareth him not. At twelve the wind fell. This was the most glorious day which I have hitherto seen.
Feb. 6th.—(The oldest sailors say they have never seen so fierce a storm as the one we had last night. The wind came from all sides at once, lifted the water from the sea, bore it through the air and cast it on the other ship, where Baron von Reck and the Salzburgers were, and so flooded it that twelve persons were kept at the pumps all night.—Dober's Diary.)	Jan. 26th.—We enjoyed the calm. I can conceive no difference comparable to that between a smooth and a rough sea, except that which is between a mind calmed by the love of God, and one torn up by the storms of earthly passion.

Nitschmann's—Continued.

Feb. 8th.—(There was a calm, and very fine weather, so that a boat could be lowered to visit the other ship.—Dober's Diary.)

Feb. 9th.—(The wind was again favorable to us, but there was much lightning.—Dober's Diary.)

Feb. 10th.—The whole day was stormy, and all night the waves broke over the ship.

Feb. 12th.—(We were obliged to drift, because we did not know how far we were from land. About noon we sighted three ships, sailed toward them, and saw they were English; our sailors lowered the boat, we

Wesley's—Continued.

Jan. 28th.—(Being a calm day, I went on board the other ship, read prayers, and visited the people. At my return I acquainted Mr. Oglethorpe with their state, and he sent them such things as they needed.—Ingham's Journal.)

Jan. 29th.—About seven in the evening we fell in with the skirts of a hurricane. The rain as well as the wind was extremely violent. The sky was so dark in a moment, that the sailors could not so much as see the ropes, or set about furling the sails. The ship must, in all probability, have overset, had not the wind fell as suddenly as it rose.

Jan. 30th.—We had another storm, which did us no other harm than splitting the foresail. Our bed being wet, I laid me down on the floor and slept sound till morning.

Feb. 1st, Sunday.—(Three sails appearing, we made up toward them, and got what letters we could write, in hopes some of them might be bound for England. One of them, that was bound for London,

Nitschmann's—Continued.
wrote in haste, and sent letters to Herrnhut. The ships came from Charlestown, and told us we were thirty hours' run from Georgia.—Dober's Diary.)

Feb. 13th.—To-day we had another storm, and twice saw the ocean not far from us, drawn up like smoke, so that the water reached up to the clouds, and the ship would have been in great danger if it had struck us.

Feb. 14th.—Soundings toward evening showed twenty-eight fathoms of water, and we hope to see land to-morrow.

Feb. 15th.—About two o'clock we saw land. I climbed the mast, and poured out my heart to God, thanking Him, and **praying** that He would care for us in our new home. We anchored for the night.

Feb. 16th.—It was a beautiful day, and the land looked very fair. At two o'clock we reached Tybee, and were all very happy. The song service was blessed, and we thanked God with prayer and praise.

Wesley's—Continued.
made towards us, and we put our letters on board her.—Ingham's Journal.)

Feb. 4th, Wednesday.—About noon the trees were visible from the mast, and in the afternoon from the main deck. In the Evening Lesson were these words, "A great door, and effectual, is opened," O let no one shut it!

Feb. 5th.—Between two and three in the afternoon God brought us all safe into the Savannah River. We cast anchor near Tybee Island, where the grove of pines, running along the shore, made an agreeable prospect, showing, as it were, the bloom of spring in the depths of winter.

Nitschmann's—Continued.

Feb. 17th.—I went on shore with Mr. Oglethorpe, and we together fell on our knees and thanked God, and then took a boat to Savannah. I went at once to the Brethren, and we rejoiced to meet again. I found the Brethren well, and looked with wonder at what they had accomplished, went with Töltschig and Spangenberg to the garden, and also received letters from Herrnhut. Spangenberg had to go immediately to Mr. Oglethorpe to discuss many things with him.

Feb. 18th.—(About six o'clock in the evening, Br. Spangenberg came from Savannah to us, which made us very glad and thankful. He told us of the death of Br. Riedel, and held the song service, praying and thanking God for having brought us together again.—Dober's Diary.)

Feb. 19th and 20th.—(We waited for the small vessel that was to come for us. Br. Spangenberg held the prayer and song services.— Dober's Diary.)

Feb. 21st.—(The small vessel came; we had much rain, and the wind was so

Wesley's—Continued.

Feb. 6th, Friday.—About eight in the morning we first set foot on American ground. It was a small, uninhabited island, (Peeper Island), over against Tybee. Mr. Oglethorpe led us to a rising ground, where we all kneeled down to give thanks. He then took boat for Savannah. When the rest of the people were come on shore, we called our little flock together to prayers. Several parts of the Second Lesson (Mark VI.) were wonderfully suited to the occasion.

Feb. 7th.—Mr. Oglethorpe returned from Savannah with Mr. Spangenberg, one of the pastors of the Germans. I soon found what spirit he was of; and asked his advice with regard to my own conduct.

Feb. 9th.—I asked Mr. Spangenberg many questions, both concerning himself and the church at Herrnhut.

Nitschmann's—Continued.

strong against us that we had to spend the night on the transport. — Dober's Diary.)

Feb. 22nd.—(In the afternoon we reached Savannah, where we were lodged in the house which the Brethren who came a year ago have built in the town. The Lord has done all things well, and has turned to our good all that has befallen us, even when we did not understand His way, and has laid His blessing upon our journey,—thanks be unto Him.—Dober's Diary.)

Wesley's—Continued.

Feb. 16th. — Mr. Oglethorpe set out for the new settlement on the Altamahaw River. He took with him fifty men, besides Mr. Ingham, Mr. Hermsdorf, and three Indians.

Feb. 24th, Tuesday.—Mr. Oglethorpe returned. The day following I took my leave of most of the passengers of the ship. In the evening I went to Savannah.

ORGANIZATION.

The arrival of the "second company" was a marked event in the eyes of the Moravians already settled at Savannah. Hitherto all had been preparation, and labor had seemed less arduous and privations less severe because they were smoothing the path for those who were to follow, and it was with well-earned satisfaction that wives and friends were lodged in the new house, taken to the garden and the farm, and introduced to acquaintances in the town. No doubt poor Catherine Riedel's heart ached with loneliness, and her tears flowed fast, when, at the close of that long and stormy voyage, she heard of her husband's death, and stood beside his grave in the Savannah cemetery;—but there was little time for grieving in the press of matters that required attention, for Spangenberg's long visit was now to end, Nitschmann was to remain only until the organization of the Congregation was complete, and there was much to be done before these two able leaders took their departure.

Scarcely had Bishop Nitschmann greeted the members of the "first company" in the dawn of Feb. 17th, 1736, when Spangenberg and Töltschig took him to the garden two miles distant, that they might have a private and undisturbed conference. All too soon, however, word was brought that Gen. Oglethorpe wanted to see Spangenberg at once, so they retraced their steps, and Spangenberg received a hearty greeting from the General, and many compliments on what he and his party had accomplished. There is no record of the conversations among the

Moravians on that day, but they are not difficult to imagine, for the news from home and from the mission fields on the one side, and the problems and prospects in Georgia on the other, would furnish topics which many days could not exhaust.

That evening Spangenberg again called on Gen. Oglethorpe, who gave orders that a boat should take him next day to Tybee, where the ship lay at anchor, with all her passengers aboard. He also told Spangenberg about the English preacher whom he had brought over, and made inquiries about Nitschmann's position, asking that the explanation be repeated to the English preacher, who was also interested in him.

The following day Spangenberg waited upon Gen. Oglethorpe to ask about Hermsdorf, as he heard the General had promised to take him to the Altamaha, where a new town was to be built. He also begged Oglethorpe to help him arrange his departure for Pennsylvania as soon as possible, which the General agreed to do.

About six o'clock that evening Spangenberg reached the ship at Tybee, and was warmly welcomed by the Moravians, and at their song service he met the much-talked of English preacher, John Wesley. The two men liked each other at the first glance; Wesley wrote in his Journal, "I soon found what spirit he was of, and asked his advice in regard to my own conduct," while Spangenberg paralleled this in his Diary with the remark, "He told me how it was with him, and I saw that true Grace dwelt in and governed him."

During the two days which elapsed before the

transport came to take the Moravians from the ship, Wesley and Spangenberg had several long conversations, each recording the points that struck him most, but without comment. These discussions regarding doctrine and practice were renewed at intervals during the remainder of Spangenberg's stay in Savannah, and the young Englishman showed himself eager to learn the Indian language so that he might preach to the natives, generous in his offers to share his advantages of study with the Moravians, and above all determined to enforce the letter of the ecclesiastical law, as he understood it, in his new parish. He thought "it would be well if two of the Moravian women would dedicate themselves to the Indian service, and at once begin to study the language," and "as the early Church employed deaconesses, it would be profitable if these women were ordained to their office." He was also convinced "that the apostolic custom of baptism by immersion ought to be observed in Georgia." "He bound himself to no sect, but took the ground that a man ought to study the Bible and the writings of the Church Fathers of the first three centuries, accepting what agreed with these two sources, and rejecting all else." He requested the Moravians to use the Lord's Prayer at all their public services, "since this is acknowledged to have been the custom of the early Church," and since that early Church celebrated the Holy Communion every day, he thought it necessary that all members should partake at least on every Sunday. "He also had his thoughts concerning Fast days." Spangenberg promised to lay these matters before the congregation, but so far as Fast days were concerned, he said that while he would observe them as a matter of conscience if he belonged to a Church which required them, he doubted the wisdom of forcing them upon a Church in which they were not obligatory.

On the 21st, the periagua ("so they call a rather deep, large boat") came to take the Moravians to Savannah, but it was necessary to call at the other ship, as some of their baggage had been brought in that vessel. Spangenberg went ahead, and found that for some reason the baggage could not be taken off that day. He was pleasantly received by "the younger" Reck, but the Baron was absent, having gone to see the site to which the Salzburgers wished to move their settlement, Gen. Oglethorpe having given his permission. About the time the periagua arrived, a heavy rain came up, and fearing the effect on the new-comers, Spangenberg obtained permission to take them into the cabin. When ten o'clock came they decided to wait no longer, and started for Savannah, with the result that they spent the entire night in the rain, in an open boat, and then had passed but half way up the river! Early in the morning Spangenberg took two men, and his small boat and went ahead, stopping at Capt. Thomson's ship to get some things Korte had sent them from London. They reached Savannah in the afternoon, and before daybreak on Thursday, Feb. 23rd, the periagua at last landed its passengers at Savannah.

That evening Spangenberg returned with Oglethorpe to the ship, that various important matters might be more fully discussed. They agreed, (1) that the five hundred acres already surveyed for Zinzendorf should be retained, and settled, but that it would be wise to take an additional five hundred acres of more fertile land nearer Savannah, where it would be more accessible, the grant to be made to Christian Ludwig von Zinzendorf, the Count's eldest son; (2) that no Moravian could accept a fifty acre tract without pledging himself to military service, but land could be secured for a number of them at the rate of twenty acres apiece, without this obligation. This land could be selected near Zinzendorf's estate, the town to be built on the Count's property. If any wished to leave the Moravian Congregation, he should receive twenty acres elsewhere for himself. (3) Non-Moravians, like John Regnier, might live with them on the same conditions. (4) If one of the Moravians died without male issue, the Congregation should name his successor in the title to the land. (5) The promised cattle should still be given.

It was further arranged that Spangenberg should continue to hold the title to his fifty acres, but with the understanding that it was in trust for the Congregation; the same to apply to Nitschmann's land, if desired.

On the 25th and 26th, a number of Indians visited the ship, being received with much ceremony. " King " Tomochichi, and others, Spangenberg had often seen, and they were formally presented to Mr. Wesley, of whom they had heard, and to whom they gave a flask of honey and a flask of milk, with the wish that " the Great Word might be to them as milk and honey." Tomochichi told of his efforts to keep peace among the tribes, in the face of rumors that the English meant to enslave them all, and of his success so far, but he feared the Indians were not in a frame of mind to give much heed to the Gospel message. Still he welcomed the attempt, and would give what aid he could, advising that the missionaries learn the Indian tongue, and that they should not baptize,—as the Spanish did,—until the people were instructed and truly converted.

On Feb. 27th, General Oglethorpe started for the Altamaha. His journey to Georgia on this occasion had been principally to protect the southern borders of the colony by establishing two new towns on the frontier, and erecting several forts near by. One company, which sailed direct from Scotland, had landed in January, and begun a settlement at New Inverness, on the north bank of the Altamaha, and a second was now to be established on St. Simon Island, and was to be called Frederica. Oglethorpe had expected to take the Salzburgers who came on the *London Merchant,* to the southward with him, but nearly all of them decided that they preferred to join those of their number who were preparing to move to New Ebenezer, and the General did not insist, contenting himself with his English soldiers.

A periagua had been started a little in advance of the sloop which bore the provisions, arms, ammunition, and tools, and in the evening Gen. Oglethorpe followed in a swift, ten-oared boat, called,—from the service in which it was often employed,—a scout boat.

With the General went Mr. Ingham, and Lieut. Hermsdorf. The latter assured Spangenberg that he had really meant little more than to compliment the General on the occasion when he remarked "that he would ask nothing better than to follow him through bush and valley, and see him carry out his wise designs," that he did not know at that time that Oglethorpe was going to the Altamaha, nor how far away the Altamaha was. But Spangenberg gravely told him that Gen. Oglethorpe had taken his word as that of an honest man, and that he would not attempt to hold him back, only he wished him to so demean himself as to bring credit and not shame to Zinzendorf and the Moravians, to whom he was at liberty to return when he desired. Hermsdorf, therefore, went with Oglethorpe and his fifty men, was made a Captain and was given a position of importance in superintending the erection of the necessary fortifications on St. Simon.

Benjamin Ingham's visit to Frederica proved to be his first unpleasant experience in the New World. Like John Wesley, he came with the strictest ideas of Sabbath observance, etc., and as one said, in answer to a reproof, " these were new laws in America." The effect may be summed up in his own words: " My chief business was daily to visit the people, to take care of those that were sick, and to supply them with the best things we had. For a few days at the first, I had everybody's good word; but when they found I watched narrowly over them, and reproved them sharply for their faults, immediately the scene changed. Instead of blessing, came cursing, and my love and kindness were repaid with hatred and ill-will."

Oglethorpe remained on the Altamaha but a few days, and then returned to Savannah for the rest of his colonists. Meanwhile the Moravian Congregation was being fully organized. During Spangenberg's visit to Oglethorpe on his vessel, the Moravians, including Bishop Nitschmann, met together, and John Töltschig was elected manager (Vorsteher), Gottfried Haberecht, monitor (Ermahner), and Gotthard Demuth to perform various minor duties (Diener). The name of the nurse (Krankenwärter) is not given, but he was probably John Regnier, who acted as physician, not only for the Moravians, but for many of their poorer neighbors. Andrew Dober was associated with Töltschig in the management of the finances, and all of these men were solemnly inducted into office, it being the custom to give a kind of specialized ordination even for positions not commonly considered ministerial.

Three "Bands" were formed among the men,—smaller companies associated for religious improvement, each Band electing a leader charged with special oversight of the members. There was one among the married men, one among the unmarried men who were communicants, and another for the unmarried non-communicants, Töltschig, Seifert and Rose being the leaders. The women were organized in like manner, though being few in number there was probably but one Band among them, under Mrs. Töltschig who had been appointed Elderess before leaving Herrnhut. There is no reference to the celebration of the Holy Communion by the first company during their months of preparation in Savannah, nor had opportunity been given to the second company since they left the English coast, but now, with Bishop Nitschmann to preside, they were able to partake together, finding much blessing therein. They resolved in the future to commune every two weeks, but soon formed the habit, perhaps under Wesley's influence, of coming to the Lord's Table every Sunday.

When Spangenberg returned to them, a conference was held each evening, and on Sunday they had a Lovefeast, especially for those who had been selected to superintend the material and spiritual affairs of the Congregation.

On the 1st of March, John and Charles Wesley called on them, and on the 6th, Charles Wesley came again, and "opened his heart" to them. The Diary calls him "an awakened but flighty man," who had come as Gov. Oglethorpe's secretary, and was now about to go to Frederica as pastor of that turbulent flock. From him Spangenberg learned of Oglethorpe's return from Altamaha, and accompanied by Nitschmann went with him to the ship, where the Wesleys were still living. Two days were spent with Oglethorpe, who promised to give them ground containing a good bed of clay, where they could make brick, which should be sold to the Trustees' agent at 15 shillings per 1,000, two-thirds of the price to be applied on their debt, and one-third to be paid them in cash. Moreover several English boys should be apprenticed to them to learn the trade. Hemp and flax seed should also be given them, and he urged them to weave the linen, for they had men who understood the art, and cloth was scarce and dear in Georgia. He also advised them to buy oxen to use in cultivating their land; and said that they should have one-third of the grape-vines he had brought over with him, another portion was to be given to Tomochichi, the remainder to be planted in his own garden.

On the 8th, Spangenberg and Nitschmann returned to Savannah, and with Andrew Dober and John Wesley, (who had now moved from the ship,) proceeded up the river to Mrs. Musgrove's, about five miles distant. Wesley wished to select a site for a small house, which Oglethorpe had promised to build for him, where he and his companions might live while they were studying the Indian language, under Mrs. Musgrove's direction. Nitschmann wanted to visit and talk with the Indian "King," Tomochichi, and Dober was trying to find some clay suitable for pottery. The following day they returned to Savannah, and Mr. Wesley and Mr. Delamotte took up their abode with the Moravians, as Mr. Quincy, Wesley's predecessor in the Savannah pastorate, had not yet vacated his house. Wesley writes, "We had now an opportunity, day by day, of observing their whole behaviour. For we were in one room with them from morning to night, unless for the little time I spent in walking. They were always employed, always cheerful themselves, and in good humor with one another; they had put away all anger, and strife, and wrath, and bitterness, and clamor, and evil speaking; they walked worthy of the vocation wherewith they were called, and adorned the Gospel of our Lord in all things." The impression thus made upon John Wesley was lasting, and even during the subsequent years in England, when differences of every kind arose between him and the Moravians, and his Journal is full of bitter denunciations of doctrines and practices which he did not understand, and with which he was not in sympathy, he now and again interrupts himself to declare, " I can not speak of them but with tender affection, were it only for the benefits I have received from them."

An event which occurred on March 10th, is of more than local interest, in that it is the first unquestioned instance of the exercise of episcopal functions in the United States. Prior to this, and for a number of years later, clergymen of the Church of England, and English-speaking Catholic priests, were ordained in the Old World, before coming to the New, remaining under the control of the Bishop and of the Vicar Apostolic of London, while the Spanish Catholics were under the Suffragan of Santiago de Cuba, and the French Catholics under the Bishop of Quebec. Tradition mentions the secret consecration of two Bishops of Pennsylvania before this time, but its authenticity is doubted, and the two men did not exercise any episcopal powers. Therefore when Bishop Nitschmann came to Georgia, and in the presence of the Moravian Congregation at Savannah ordained one of their number to be their pastor, he was unconsciously doing one of the " first things " which are so interesting to every lover of history.

Whenever it was possible the Moravians spent Saturday afternoon and evening in rest, prayer, and conference, and on this occasion four services were held at short intervals.

DAVID NITSCHMANN (Episc.).

At the first service the singing of a hymn was followed by the reading of Psa. 84, a discourse thereon, and prayer. The second was devoted to reading letters from Germany, and some discussion as to Hermsdorf and his relation to the Congregation. The third service was the important one, and the following account was recorded in the Diary. "When we re-assembled the question: 'Must not our Congregation have a Chief Elder (Aeltester)?' was presented for discussion. All thought it necessary, and were unanimous in their choice of Anton Seifert, and no other was even suggested. While his name was being considered, he was sent from the room, and when he had been recalled, we sang a hymn, and Nitschmann and Töltschig led the Congregation in most earnest prayer. Then Nitschmann delivered an earnest charge, setting before him the importance of his office, which made him the foremost member of the Congregation, especially in times of danger, for in the early Church, as well as among our forefathers in Moravia, the bishops were ever the first victims. He was asked if he would freely and willingly give up his life for the Congregation and the Lord Jesus. He answered, 'Yes.' Then he was reminded of the evil which arose when bishops, seeing their power in a Congregation, began to exalt themselves, and to make outward show of their pre-eminence. He was asked whether he would recognize as evil, abjure, and at once suppress any inclination he might feel toward pride in his position as Chief Elder, and his larger authority. He answered with a grave and thoughtful 'Yes.' Then our Nitschmann prayed over him earnestly, and ordained him to his office with the laying on of hands. Nitschmann was uncommonly aroused and happy, but Anton Seifert was very humble and quiet." John Wesley, who was present, wrote "The great simplicity, as well as solemnity, of the whole, almost made me forget the seventeen hundred years between, and imagine myself in one of those assemblies where form and state were not; but Paul the tent-maker, or Peter the fisherman, presided; yet with the demonstration of the Spirit and of power."

Both Wesley and Benjamin Ingham refer to Seifert as a "bishop," which is a mistake, though a natural one. Wesley was present at the ordination, and heard the charge, with example and warning drawn from the actions of earlier bishops; while Ingham, in the course of several long conversations with Töltschig concerning the Moravian Episcopate and Seifert's ordination, asked "is Anton a bishop?" and was answered, "yes, *for our Congregation.*" This was in view of the fact that Bishop Nitschmann, in ordaining Seifert, had empowered him to delegate another member to hold the Communion, baptize, or perform the marriage ceremony in case of his sickness or necessary absence. At that time the Moravian Church was just beginning to form her own ministry, the ranks of Deacon, Presbyter and Bishop were not fully organized, and the definite system was only established by the Tenth General Synod of the Church in 1745. The exigencies of the case required large powers for a man serving in an isolated field, and they were given him, but strictly speaking, Seifert was only ordained a Deacon, and never was consecrated Bishop.

The fourth and last service of the day was given up to song, a discourse, and prayer.

On Sunday, March 11th, after morning prayers, Wesley went to Tybee for an interview with General Oglethorpe. At a general gathering of the Moravians later in the day, the second chapter of Acts was read, with special reference to the last four verses, and the description of the first congregation of Christ's followers, when "all that believed were together, and had all things common," was taken as the pattern of their "Gemeinschaft." This plan, which had already been tested during the first year, proved so advantageous that it was later adopted by other American Moravian settlements, being largely responsible for their rapid growth during their early years, though in each case there came a time when it hindered further progress, and was therefore abandoned. In religious matters, the organization of the Savannah Congregation had been modeled after that at Herrnhut, so far as possible, but in material things the circumstances were very different. At Herrnhut the estates of Count Zinzendorf, under the able supervision of the Countess, were made to pay practically all the general Church expenses, and many of the members were in the service of the Saxon nobleman, Nicholas Lewis, Count Zinzendorf, in various humble positions, even while in the Church he divested himself of his rank and fraternized with them as social equals. But the men who emigrated to Georgia had undertaken to support themselves and carry on a mission work, and Spangenberg, with his keen insight, grasped the idea that a common purpose warranted a community of service, the labor of all for the benefit of all, with every duty, no matter how menial, done as unto the Lord, whom they all, in varying degrees, acknowledged as their Master. Later, in Bethlehem, Pa., with a larger number of colonists, and wider interests to be subserved, Spangenberg again introduced the plan, and elaborated it into a more or less intricate system, which is described in a clear and interesting manner in "A History of Bethlehem," by Rt. Rev. J. Mortimer Levering, which has recently been published.

Not only on account of its successor the "Oeconomie," at Bethlehem, and others copied therefrom, but in view of the various modern attempts which have been and are still being made to demonstrate that the action of the early Church at Jerusalem can be duplicated and made financially successful, it is worth while to rescue the resolutions of the Moravian Congregation at Savannah from the oblivion of the manuscript Diary, in which they have been so long concealed, noting the claim that this was the first time since Apostolic days, that a Congregation had formed itself into such a "Society,"— a "Gemeinschaft."

"In our gathering we read Acts II, and spoke of the *Gemeinschaft,* for we are planning to work, to sow and reap, and to suffer with one another. This will be very useful, for many a man who has not understood or exerted himself, will by this means see himself and be led to improve. Others also will see from it that we love each other, and will glorify the Father in Heaven. There has been no "society" like that at Jerusalem, but at this present time it becomes necessary, for material reasons. Were we only individuals all would fear to give one of us credit, for they would think, 'he might die,' but nothing will be denied the 'Society,' for each stands for the other. Each member must work diligently, since he does not labor for himself alone but for his brethren, and this will prevent much laziness. No one must rely on the fact that he understands a handicraft, and so on, for there is a curse on him who relies on human skill and forgets the Divine power. No one will be pressed to give to the 'Society' any property which has hitherto belonged to him.—Each person present was asked if he had any remarks to make, but there were no objections raised. Moreover the brethren were told that if one should fall so low that he not only withdrew himself from the brethren, but was guilty of gross sin, he would be forced to work for another master until he had earned enough to pay his transportation here and back again, for we would not willingly permit such a man to remain in the land as an offence to the Indians."

It is interesting to observe that care for the poor Indians is the argument given for the course to be pursued in dealing with a recreant member! They had come to preach the Gospel to the Indians, and did not propose that evil should be learned through fault of theirs.

At his earnest request, John Regnier was now admitted to the "Society," his presence among them so far having been without distinct agreement as to his standing. This did not make him a communicant member of the Church, simply put him on a par with the other non-communicants, of whom there were quite a number in the Congregation.

In the evening Anton Seifert, so recently ordained Chief Elder, or pastor, of the Congregation, officiated for the first time at a Confirmation service, the candidate being Jacob Frank. He had been in poor health when the second company left Germany, and Count Zinzendorf had advised him not to go, but his heart was set on it, and he would not be persuaded. He grew worse during the voyage and was now very ill with dropsy, but in such a beautiful Christian spirit that no one could deny his wish for full membership in the Church. Having given satisfactory answers to the searching questions put to him, the blessing was laid upon his head, and he expressed so great a desire to partake of the Lord's Supper that his request was immediately granted, the Elders and Helpers (Helfer) communing with him. Two or three days later he asked Spangenberg to write his will, and then his strength gradually failed, until on March 19th, he "passed to the Lord," leaving to his associates the remembrance of his willing and happy departure.

The term "Helpers" was used to express in a general way all those, both men and women, who were charged with the spiritual and temporal affairs of the Congregation. Many of the words employed as official titles by the Moravians were given a specialized significance which makes it difficult to find an exact English equivalent for them, though they are always apt when the meaning is understood. Perhaps the best example of this is "Diener," which means "servant," according to the dictionary, and was used to designate those who "served" the Congregation in various ways. Until quite recently a Lovefeast, held annually in Salem, N. C., for members of Church Boards, Sunday-School Teachers, Church Choir, Ushers, etc. was familiarly known as "the Servants' Lovefeast," a direct inheritance from the earlier days. It is now more commonly called "the Workers' Lovefeast," an attempt to unite "Helper" and "Diener" in a term understood by all.

At a "Helpers' Conference" held on March 13th, it was decided to have nothing more to do with Vollmar, the Wittenberg carpenter, who had crossed with the second company, had proved false and malicious, and had now joined Herr von Reck's party without the consent of the Moravians. More important, however, than the Vollmar affair, was the proposed departure of Spangenberg for Pennsylvania. Most faithfully had he fulfilled his commission to take the first company of Moravians to Georgia, and settle them there, patiently had he labored for and with them during their days of greatest toil and privation, controlling his own desire to keep his promise and go to the Schwenkfelders, who were complaining with some bitterness of his broken faith; but now his task was ended, the Savannah Congregation was ready to be thrown on its own resources, Gen. Oglethorpe had provided him with letters of introduction, and the "lot" said, "Let him go, for the Lord is with him."

Final questions were asked and answered, Spangenberg's Commission was delivered to him, and then Bishop Nitschmann "laid his blessing upon" him. In the Lutheran Church, to which he belonged before he joined the Moravians, Spangenberg had been an accredited minister of the Gospel. The Church of England refused to acknowledge the validity of Lutheran ordination, because that Church had no Episcopate, but the Moravians, influenced by Count Zinzendorf, himself a Lutheran by birth, broad-minded, liberal, and devout, did not hesitate to fraternize with the Lutherans, or even to accept the Sacraments at the hands of Pastor Rothe, in charge of the Parish Church of Berthelsdorf. At the same time they prized the Episcopate lately transferred to them from the ancient Unitas Fratrum, and while continuing in free fellowship with Christians of all denominational names, they now intended to so ordain their own ministry that no church could question it. When the three grades were established in 1745, a license to preach granted by the Lutheran Church was considered equivalent to the rank of Deacon, ordination in the Moravian Church making the minister a Presbyter.

Now fully equipped for his mission to the English Colony of Pennsylvania, Spangenberg left Savannah on March 15th, going on Capt. Dunbar's ship to Port Royal, where he lodged with a man who was born in Europe, his wife in Africa, their child in Asia, and they were all now living in America! From Port Royal he went by land almost to Charlestown, the last short distance being in a chance boat, and from Charlestown he sailed to New York.

From there he proceeded to Philadelphia, and to the Schwenkfelders, making his home with Christopher Wiegner on his farm in the Skippack woods, where George Böhnisch was also living. Spangenberg worked on the farm that he might not be a burden to his host, and might meet the neighbors in a familiar way, meanwhile making numerous acquaintances, and gaining much valuable information.

Bishop Nitschmann remained in Savannah until March 26th, when he sailed to Charlestown. There he was detained ten days waiting for a northbound ship, and employed the time in delivering several letters of introduction, and learning all he could about Carolina, and the conditions there. On the 28th of April he reached New York, and left on the 9th of May for Philadelphia, going partly by boat, and partly on foot, reaching there on the 13th. Six weeks he and Spangenberg spent together, visiting many neighborhoods, and informing themselves as to the religious and material outlook in Pennsylvania, and then Nitschmann sailed for Germany.

His report gave a new turn to the American plans, for both he and Spangenberg were much pleased with Pennsylvania. Quite a number of the settlers seemed open to the idea of mutual aid in the spiritual life, material conditions were very different from those in Georgia and better suited to the Moravian needs, the Quaker Governor was not likely to force military service upon people who held the same theories as himself in regard to warfare, and there were large tribes of Indians within easy reach, to whom the Gospel might be preached. As troubles thickened in Savannah, therefore, the heads of the Church at Herrnhut began to look toward Pennsylvania, and ultimately sent thither the larger companies originally destined for Georgia.

In August, Spangenberg went to visit the Moravian Mission on the island of St. Thomas, returning to Pennsylvania in November, where he remained until the following year.

CHAPTER V.

THE SECOND YEAR IN GEORGIA.

THE ENGLISH CLERGYMEN.

The same day that Bishop Nitschmann left Savannah, John Wesley, moved into the parsonage which had just been vacated by his predecessor, Mr. Quincy. A week earlier he had entered upon his ministry at Savannah, being met by so large and attentive an audience that he was much encouraged, and began with zeal to perform his pastoral duties. He was the third Rector of the Savannah Parish, the Rev. Henry Herbert having been the first, and he preached in a rude chapel built on the lot reserved for a house of worship in the original plan of Savannah,—the site of the present Christ Church.

The first word of discouragement was brought by Ingham, who returned from Frederica on April 10th, with a message from Charles Wesley begging his brother to come to his relief. He told a woeful story of persecution by the settlers, and injustice from Oglethorpe to Charles Wesley, all undeserved, as Oglethorpe freely admitted when he threw off the weight of suspicion laid upon his mind by malicious slanderers, and sought an interview with his young secretary, in which much was explained and forgiven. But poor Charles was in great straits when he sent Ingham to Savannah, sick, slighted, and abused, deprived even of the necessaries of life, and so cast down that on one occasion he exclaimed, "Thanks be to God, it is not yet made a capital offence to give me a morsel of bread!"

Wesley obeyed the summons, taking Delamotte with him, Ingham caring for the Church and Delamotte's school during their absence. There were poor school facilities in Savannah prior to Delamotte's arrival, and he at once saw the need, and devoted himself to it. Delamotte seems to have been a quiet man, who took little share in the aggressive work of his companions, and consequently escaped the abuse which was heaped upon them.

On April 22nd, Ingham sent an invitation to Töltschig to visit him, and this was the beginning of a close personal friendship which lasted for the rest of their lives, and of such a constant intercourse between Ingham and the Moravian Church, that he is often supposed to have become a member of it, though he really never severed his connection with the Church of England. Töltschig speaks of him as "a very young man, about 24 or 25 years of age, who has many good impulses in his soul, and is much awakened." He had come to Georgia for the sole purpose of bearing the Gospel message to the Indians, and it was through him that the Moravians were finally able to begin their missionary work.

When Wesley and Delamotte returned from Frederica, the former resumed his association with the Moravians, continuing to join in their Sunday evening service, and translating some of their hymns into English.

In May two questions were asked of Töltschig, upon the answering of which there depended more than any one imagined. The Diary says,—"The 20th, was Sunday.—Mr. Ingham asked if we could not recognize and receive him as our brother; to which I replied, that he did not know us well enough, nor we him, we must first understand each other better. On the 21st, Mr. Wesley spoke with me, and asked me the selfsame question. I said to him that we had seen much of him day by day, and that it was true that he loved us and we loved him, but that we did not so quickly admit any one into our Congregation." Then at his request Töltschig outlined the Moravian view of conversion, and the requisites for church-membership.

A few days later Charles Wesley unexpectedly returned from Frederica, and Oglethorpe sent word that either John Wesley or Ingham should come down in his place. The latter was by no means anxious to go,—his former experience had not been agreeable, but the reason he gave the Moravians was that a number of Indian traders were soon to visit Savannah, and he was very anxious to see them. They advised him to be guided by John Wesley's wish, which he agreed to do, and then found that Wesley had decided to go himself.

During the weeks that followed, Ingham and Charles Wesley were frequently with Töltschig, who answered as best he could their many questions regarding the history of the Moravian Episcopate, a matter of vital importance to a strict member of the Church of England who was thinking of allying himself with them. Everything they heard confirmed Ingham in his intention, and when John Wesley returned in July he and Ingham again made application "to be received as brethren in our Congregation, and to go with us to the Lord's Table. We entirely refused to admit them into the Congregation, and I (Töltschig) gave them the reasons therefor: (1) That we did not know them well enough; (2) and that they perhaps did not know us well enough, both things which we considered highly important; and (3) that their circumstances and situation were such that it would be difficult if not impossible for them to comply with the requirements of such admission." The promises expected from a Confirmand,—to which they also must have bound themselves,—are thus summarized. "To give body and soul to the Lord now and forever; to devote and dedicate himself to the service of the Unity, according to the grace and gifts bestowed on him by the Saviour; and willingly to submit to the discipline and regulations which the Unity has established for the welfare and improvement of souls." Could these two men, in the zeal and vigor of their youth, honestly have made these promises, the Moravian Church would have gained two invaluable co-workers, but they seem to have accepted Töltschig's argument as conclusive, and dropped the matter, with no ill-will or disturbance of the existing pleasant relations.

Concerning the Communion "we assured them that we loved them, and would welcome them as honored guests at the Lord's Supper, for we believed that they loved the Lord." This invitation, however, the young clergymen would not accept.

On the 6th of August, Charles Wesley left for England, bearing dispatches to the Trustees, and with the hope of interesting others in the evangelizing of the Indians. He meant himself to return to Georgia, but feeble health prevented, and he resigned his office as Secretary to Gen. Oglethorpe the following May. His brother John accompanied him to Charlestown, and then went to Frederica to deliver certain letters to Gen. Oglethorpe. He found there was "less and less prospect of doing good at Frederica, many there being extremely zealous, and indefatigably diligent to prevent it," his opposers even attempting personal violence. One "lady" tried to shoot him, and when he seized her hands and took away her pistol, she maliciously bit a great piece out of his arm. Still he made two more visits to the place, and then in "utter despair of doing good there," took his final leave of Frederica.

WORK AMONG THE INDIANS.

When the Moravians adopted the conversion of the Indians as their main object for settling in America, they were greatly influenced by the attractive descriptions of the "wild people" which were being published. In a "Report," ascribed to Gen. Oglethorpe, it is stated that "nothing is lacking for their conversion to the Christian faith except a knowledge of their language, for they already have an admirable conception of *morals*, and their conduct agrees perfectly therewith. They have a horror of adultery, and disapprove of polygamy. Thieving is unknown to them. Murder is considered an abominable crime, and no one may be killed except an enemy, when they esteem it a virtue." This, like too many a description written then and now to exploit a colonizing scheme, was far too good to be true. The Indians proved apt learners, but of the vices rather than the virtues of the English, and drunkenness with all its attendant evils, was quickly introduced. Afraid of their dusky neighbors, anxious to keep on good terms with them, distrusting their loyalty to the English under the bribes offered by French and Spanish, the Government tried to limit the intercourse between the Indians and the settlers as much as possible, treating the former as honored guests whenever they came to Savannah, but forbidding the latter to go to them without special permit in times of peace, and not at all in time of war.

When the Moravians came the restlessness which presaged war was stirring among the tribes, becoming more and more pronounced, and one of the Indian Chiefs said frankly, "Now our enemies are all about us, and we can do nothing but fight, but if the Beloved Ones should ever give us to be at peace, then we would hear the Great Word."

Tomochichi, indeed, bade the missionaries welcome, and promised to do all in his power to gain admission for them into all parts of his nation, but the time was not ripe, nor was his influence equal to his good-will. Though called a "king," he was only chief of a small tribe living some four or five miles from Savannah, part of the Creek Confederacy, which was composed of a number of remnants, gradually merged into one "nation." The "Upper

TOMO CHACHI MICO
oder König Von Yamacran und Tooanahowi Seines Bruders
des Mico oder Königes Von Etichitas Sohn.
nach dem Londischen Original in Augspurg nachgestochen
von
Joh Jacob Kleinschmidt.

Creeks" lived about the head waters of the creeks from which they took their name, and the "Lower Creeks," including Tomochichi's people, were nearer the sea-coast. Ingham, whose heart was set on the Indian work, was at first very anxious to go to the Cherokees, who lived near the mountains, at a considerable distance from Savannah, having been told that they had a desire to hear the "Great Word." On April 22nd, he spoke of his wish to Töltschig, inviting Seifert and, if they chose, another Moravian to join him in the work. It was the best opportunity that had yet offered, and Seifert wanted to go to the Indians, having already studied their language as best he could, but they hesitated to undertake the work conjointly with Ingham. After some time the Cherokee plan was abandoned. Oglethorpe objected on account of the danger that they would be intercepted and killed, it being a fourteen day land journey to reach the Cherokee country, and he positively refused to let John Wesley go because that would leave Savannah without a minister. Töltschig says Wesley's interest in the Indian work failed, and another writer says he gave up the work because he could not learn the Indian language, but Wesley lays all the blame on Oglethorpe.

In January, 1737, the question of going to the Upper Creeks was submitted to the "lot," and the Moravians were bidden to wait for another opening. Meanwhile an actual beginning had been made among the Lower Creeks. On the 7th of May, Ingham and John Wesley went up the river to the home of Mrs. Musgrove, the half-breed woman who at this time was of such great use as interpreter and mediator between the Indians and the English. Arrangements were made by which Ingham should spend three days of each week with her, teaching her children to read in exchange for instruction in the Indian language. The other three or four days were to be spent in Savannah, communicating to Wesley the knowledge he had acquired, Anton Seifert sharing in the lessons.

On the 19th of June, the Moravians held a meeting to determine whether the time had come for them to take up the Indian work in earnest. The "lot" was appealed to, and the answer being that the language should be learned, Seifert, George Neisser and John Böhner were appointed to make diligent use of Ingham's instructions. The frequent visits of Tomochichi and his people to Savannah gave them an opportunity to practice speaking, for the Moravan house was always open to the red men, and food and drink were theirs at any time of day, a fact of which the visitors were not slow to take advantage.

The "lot" had so great an influence on the progress of affairs in the Moravian Congregation at Savannah from this time on that it is necessary to understand how the institution was regarded. The use of the lot was common in Old Testament days; and in the New Testament it is recorded that when an apostle was to be chosen to take the place of the traitor, Judas, the lot decided between two men who had been selected as in every way suited for the place. Following this example the members of the ancient Unitas Fratrum used the lot in the selection of their first ministers, and the Renewed Church did the same when the first elders were elected at Herrnhut in 1727. It was no uncommon practice in Germany, where many persons who desired special guidance resorted to it more or less freely, and Count Zinzendorf, among the rest, had used it from his youth up. Gradually it came into general use among the Moravians, and at a later period in their history had its definite place in their system of government, though the outside public never fully understood it, and still holds erroneous views, despite the plain statements that have been made. By degrees its use became more and more restricted, and has been long since entirely abolished.

In its perfection the lot was simply this,—human intellect solving a problem so far as earnest study and careful deliberation could go, and then, if the issue was still in doubt, a direct appeal for Divine guidance, in perfect faith that the Lord would plainly answer his servants, who were seeking to do his will. This standard was not always maintained, but the leaders of the Moravian Congregation in Savannah had the early, absolute, belief that God spoke to them through the lot, and felt themselves bound to implicit obedience to its dictates. Their custom was to write two words or sentences on separate slips, representing the two possible answers to their question, and after earnest prayer to draw one slip, and then act accordingly. Sometimes a third slip, a blank, was added, and if that was drawn it signified that no action should be taken until another time, and after further consideration.

Some time in July, Peter Rose and his wife, (the widow Riedel) went to live among the Lower Creeks, giving all their time to learning the language, and teaching what they could about religion.

On August 9th, Mr. Ingham went to the Moravians with a new plan. Gen. Oglethorpe had agreed to build a schoolhouse for Indian children, near Tomochichi's village, with the idea that it would give opportunity also to reach the older men and women with the Gospel message. The house was to contain three rooms, one for Ingham, one for the Moravian missionaries, and one to be used for the school, and it was suggested that the Moravians undertake the erection of the building, the Trustees' fund to pay them for their labor. The proposition was gladly accepted, and preparations were at once made to send the necessary workmen.

On Monday, the 13th, Töltschig and five others went to the spot which had been selected for the Indian Schoolhouse, usually called *Irene*. The site of this schoolhouse has been considered uncertain, but a short manuscript account of "the Mission among the Indians in America," preserved in the Herrnhut Archieves, says distinctly that it stood "a mile above the town (of Savannah) on an island in the Savannah River which was occupied by the Creeks."

When the carpenters arrived the first act was to unite in prayer for a blessing on their work, and then they began to fell trees and cut down bushes, clearing the ground for the hut in which they were to live while building the schoolhouse. The hut was placed on the grave of an Indian chief. "The

Indians are accustomed to bury their chiefs on the spot where they died, to heap a mound some 24 feet high above them, to mourn them for a while, and then to abandon the spot," and this little elevation was a favorable site for their hut. Until the hut was finished the men lodged with the Indians, Tomochichi himself taking charge of their belongings. Töltschig returned the same day to Savannah, going back later with a supply of provisions. The Indians made them heartily welcome to their neighborhood, and the Moravians, even in the midst of their building operations, began to teach them the English alphabet, at the same time putting forth every effort to learn the Indian tongue, in which Rose was rapidly becoming proficient.

By the 20th of September the schoolhouse was finished, and Ingham and the Moravians held a conference to plan the future work, and decide what duties each should assume, as he proposed to move thither at once, and, with the approval of the lot, Rose and his wife were to do the same. Morning and evening they were to read the English Bible, accompanied by silent prayer; morning, mid-day and evening an hour was to be given to the study of the Indian language; and Rose and his wife were to have an hour for their private devotions. Mrs. Rose was to teach the Indian girls to read, and the boys, who had already begun to read, were to be taught to write. In their remaining time they were to clear and plant some land, that they might not be too long dependent on the Congregation at Savannah, and on the friendly Indians, who were giving them much.

The next day Mr. and Mrs. Töltschig escorted Rose and his wife to their new home, and at Ingham's request united with them in a little prayer service. Four days later fourteen of the Moravians went to the schoolhouse, which was solemnly consecrated by Seifert, the Chief Elder. That evening, in Savannah, Rose and his wife were formally set apart for their missionary work, and the next day they returned to "Irene," as the school was called, to enter upon their duties.

At first everything was encouraging. The children learned readily, not only to read but some to write; they committed to memory many passages of Scripture, and took special delight in the hymns they were taught to sing.

The older Indians looked on with wonder and approval, which stimulated the missionaries to new zeal in mastering the language, and in taking every opportunity to make the "Great Word" known to them. Zinzendorf wrote a letter from Herrnhut to Tomochichi, commending his interest in their message, and urging its full acceptance upon him; the Indians gave some five acres of land for a garden, which Rose cleared and planted, and everything looked promising, until the influence of the Spanish war rumor was felt. True to their nature, the fighting spirit of the Indians rose within them, and they took the war-path against the Spanish, for the sake of their English allies, and perhaps more for the pure love of strife. Then Ingham decided to go to England for reinforcements, and Rose was left in charge of the work. He seems to have been a well-meaning man, and much beloved by the Indians, but he was not a man of much mental strength or executive ability, and the Congregation at Savannah soon decided that he and his wife should be recalled until the way opened for one or more of the others to go back to Irene with him.

THE "SOCIETY."

In their personal affairs the Moravians were experiencing the usual mingling of light and shadow.

Dober's effort to make pottery was a failure, for lack of proper clay, but through Gen. Oglethorpe's kindness a good deal of carpenter's work was given to them. They built a house for Tomochichi at his village, and a house in Savannah, both in the style of the Moravian house, and another town house in English fashion, as well as the Indian school, a large share of their wages being applied on account, so that their debt was gradually reduced, and their credit sustained.

Their manner of living remained very simple. Morning and evening prayers began and ended their days of toil, the company being divided, part living at the garden, and part in town during the week, all gathering in the town-house for Sunday's rest and worship. When the weather was very warm the morning Bible reading was postponed until the noon hour, that advantage might be taken of the cooler air for active labor. Once a month a general conference was held on Saturday evening, with others as needed, so that all might do the work for which they were best fitted, and which was most necessary at the time. "Who worked much gave much, who worked less gave less, who did not work because he was sick or weak gave nothing into the common fund; but when they needed food, or drink, or clothing, or other necessary thing, one was as another."

On the 3rd of April, Matthias Seybold asked to be received into the communicant Congregation, which was done on the 5th of May, and he shared in the Lord's Supper for the first time June 3rd. John Böhner also was confirmed on January 12th of the following year.

On the 11th of November two little girls, Anna and Comfort, were added to their household. The mother had recently died, and the father offered to pay the Moravians for taking care of them, but they preferred to have them bound, so they could not be taken away just when they had begun to learn, and so it was arranged. On the 28th, a man from Ebenezer brought his son, and apprenticed him to Tanneberger, the shoemaker.

The dark side of the picture arose from two causes, ill health, and matrimonial affairs. There was a great deal of sickness throughout Georgia that summer, and the second company became acclimated through the same distressing process that the first had found so hard to bear. Mrs. Dober, Mrs. Waschke, Mrs. Töltschig, Gottlieb Demuth, John Böhner and others were sick at various times, and David Jag cut his foot so severely that he was unable to use it for four months. Nor was this the worst, for three more of their number died. Roscher was sick when he reached Savannah, with consumption, it was supposed, but Regnier suspected that this was not all, and when Roscher died, March 30th, he secured permission to make an autopsy, in which he was assisted by John Wesley. The examination showed a large hematoma in the left wall of the abdomen, and other complications. The records say, "we have no cause to grieve over his departure, for he was a good soul," and died in peace.

The next to pass away was Mrs. Haberecht. Her health began to fail the latter part of March, but she did not become seriously ill until the 26th of May, when she returned from the farm, where she and others had been employed, and told her friends that the Saviour had called her, and her end was near. With joy and peace she waited for the summons, which was delayed for some time, though on several occasions her death seemed only a matter of hours. On the 16th of June she shared with the others in the celebration of the Communion, and on the following evening "went to the Saviour."

Matthias Böhnisch's illness was of short duration, lasting only from the 27th of September to the 3rd of October. He had had a severe fall on the ship coming over, from which he continued to suffer, and now a hard blow on the chest injured him mortally. Some of his companions found it hard to understand why he should be taken, for he was a good man, who gave promise of much usefulness in the Lord's service. It is an old question, often asked and never fully answered, but Böhnisch, conscious almost to the last, was perfectly willing to go, and his associates felt that the influence of his life "would be a seed, which would bear fruit" in others.

It was a serious mistake that sent Juliana Jäschke to Savannah with the second company. A seamstress was badly needed, and had she been so minded she might have been very useful, but in a list giving very briefly the standing of each one in the "Society," it is curtly stated that she was "ill-mannered, and obstructing everything." Soon after her arrival it was suggested that she marry Peter Rose, but the lot forbade and he found a much better helpmeet in the widow of Friedrich Riedel. Waschke thought he would like to marry Juliana, but she refused, even though Bishop Nitschmann, Mr. and Mrs. Töltschig pled with her. Her preference was for George Haberland, and the result was an uncomfortable state of affairs, which disturbed the leaders of the "Society" not a little, for living as they did as one large family it meant constant friction on all sides. They did not know whether to force Juliana to submit to their authority, (as a member of the "Society" she had pledged herself to obedience to the duly elected officers), or whether they should wait and hope for a better frame of mind. At last they referred it to the lot, which read "Juliana shall not marry any one yet." This settled the question for the time being, but did not improve the spirit of the parties concerned. A few of the others were homesick, and lost interest in their work and the cause for which they had come over. Hermsdorf returned from Frederica, sick and depressed, and was kindly received by the Moravians in Savannah, though their first favorable impression of him had been lost on the voyage across the

Atlantic, when he complained of the fare, and lay in bed most of the time.

The leaders of the party, trying to pacify the discontented, comfort the sick, and strengthen those that were left as one and another was called away; planning the daily routine to the best advantage so that they might repay their debt, and still have the necessaries of life for their large company; seeking to teach and convert the Indians, and help the poor about them;—these leaders were further tried by the non-arrival of answers to the letters sent to Germany. Feeling that they *must* know the will of those at home if they were to be able successfully to continue their work, they at last decided to send a messenger to Count Zinzendorf, and the lot designated Andrew Dober.

A ship was lying at anchor, ready to take Gen. Oglethorpe to England, and he readily agreed to take Dober and wife with him, and on December 2nd, they embarked, Dober carrying a number of letters and papers. Mrs. Dober was quite ill when they left, but rapidly improved in the sea breezes. January 20th, the ship reached London, and Mr. and Mrs. Dober went at once to Mr. Weintraube, who was to forward the letters to Herrnhut. As they were talking Bishop Nitschmann walked in, to their mutual great astonishment. He reported that Count Zinzendorf had just arrived in London, and had sent to inquire for letters, so those brought from Georgia were at once delivered. Zinzendorf rented a house, the Countess arrived a few days later, and Dober and wife remained in his service during the seven weeks of his stay.

The Count's object in visiting London at this time was fourfold: to confer with the Georgia Trustees about the Moravians in Savannah; to extend acquaintances among the Germans in London and do religious work among them; to discuss the Episcopate of the Unitas Fratrum with Archbishop Potter of Canterbury; and if possible to revive the "Order of the Mustard Seed." This order had been established by Zinzendorf and several companions in their early boyhood, and grew with their growth, numbering many famous men in its ranks, and it is worthy of note that even in its boyish form it contained the germs of that zeal for missions which was such a dominant feature of the Count's manhood.

Archbishop Potter not only fully acknowledged the validity of the Unity's Episcopate, but urged Zinzendorf himself to accept consecration at the hands of Jablonski and David Nitschmann, and encouraged by him Zinzendorf was consecrated bishop at Berlin, May 20th, 1737.

The Count held frequent services during his stay in London, and before he left a society of ten members had been formed among the Germans, with a few simple regulations, their object being "in simplicity to look to these three things:—to be saved by the blood of Christ; to become holy, or be sanctified by the blood of Christ; to love one another heartily."

With the Trustees it was agreed: "That the Count's men" might remain for two years longer at Savannah, without cultivating the five hundred acre tract, "and be exempt from all forfeitures arising from such non-cultivation;" but if they chose they

NICHOLAS LEWIS, COUNT ZINZENDORF.
Portrait Bust by Reichel, Berlin.

THE SECOND YEAR IN GEORGIA. 161

might move to the tract any time during the two years. They might go to Tomochichi's Indians whenever they saw fit and he consented. Other Indians could not be visited in time of war, but in peace four Moravians should be licensed to go to them, on the same footing as the English ministers. Those living with Tomochichi were not included in this number. "As the Moravian Church is believed to be orthodox and apostolic" no one should interfere with their preaching the Gospel, or prevent the Indians from attending their services in Savannah, or elsewhere. The title to their five hundred acre tract was secured to the Moravians, even in case the Count's male line should become extinct.

Reference to military service is conspicuous by its absence, and at the very time that these resolutions were being framed, assurance on that one point was being desperately needed in Savannah.

RUMORS OF WAR.

In February, 1737, that which Spangenberg had feared came upon the Moravians,—military service was peremptorily demanded of them, the occasion being a fresh alarm of Spanish incursions.

The feud between the colonists of Spain and England was of long standing, dating back to rival claims to the New World by right of discovery. The English asserted that through the Cabots they had a right to the greater part of North America, and a grant to the Lords Proprietors of Carolina, in 1663, named the 31 degree of latitude as the southern boundary. Another patent two years later set the line at the 29 degree, but that availed nothing as it included the northern part of Florida, where the Spanish were already settled in considerable numbers.

No other nation questioned the English claim to the sea-board as far as the 31 degree, which was well south of the Altamaha, but the Spanish greatly resented the settlements in Carolina, as encroaching on their territory, though successive treaties between the two Governments had virtually acknowledged the English rights. With the two nations nominally at peace, the Spanish incited the Indians to deeds of violence, encouraged insurrection among the negro slaves, welcomed those who ran away, and enlisted them in their army. Now and then the Governor of Carolina would send a force, which would subdue them for a time, but the constant uncertainty made Carolina welcome the Georgia colony as a protection to her borders.

The settlement of Georgia gave further offense to Spain, and her subjects in Florida burned to exterminate the intruders, as they considered them, though nothing was done so long as operations were confined to the Savannah River. But when towns and forts were planned and begun on the Altamaha their opposition became more outspoken. Oglethorpe did all he could to preserve peace without retreating from his position, and in Oct. 1736, he concluded a treaty with the Governor of St. Augustine.

Only too soon it became apparent that this treaty would not be respected, for the Captain-General of Cuba disapproved, and Oglethorpe sailed for England, in November, to urge the immediate and sufficient fortification of the frontier. The Trustees and the Government approved of the course he had pursued, but Spain recalled and executed the Governor of St. Augustine, for presuming to make such a treaty, and so plainly showed her intention to make war on Georgia that the English Government authorized Oglethorpe to raise a regiment for service there, and in July, 1738, he sailed for America, commissioned to take command of all the military forces of Carolina and Georgia, and protect the colonies.

During the nineteen months of his absence, the Georgia colonists were in a continual state of uneasiness, which now and then became sheer panic at some especially plausible report of imminent danger.

On February 17th, 1737, Mr. Causton received a letter from Charlestown, in which the Governor informed him that he had news of the approach of the Spaniards, and Savannah at once became excited, and prepared for defence. On the 20th, officers went through the town, taking the names of all who could bear arms, freeholders and servants alike. Three of them came to the Moravian house and requested names from Töltschig. He answered "there was no one among them who could bear arms, and he would get no names from them." They said, "it was remarkable that in a house full of strong men none could bear arms,—he should hurry and give them the names, they could not wait." Töltschig answered, "if they wanted to go no one would stop them, there would be no names given." They threatened to tell Mr. Causton,

Töltschig approved, and said he would do the same, and they angrily left the house.

Ingham accompanied Töltschig to Mr. Causton, who at once began to argue the matter, and a spirited debate ensued, of which the following is a résumé. *Causton.* "Everybody must go to the war and fight for his own safety, and if you will not join the army the townspeople will burn down your house, and will kill you all."

Töltschig. "That may happen, but we can not help it, it is against our conscience to fight."

Causton. "If you do not mean to fight you had better go and hide in the woods, out of sight of the people, or it will be the worse for you; and you had better go before the enemy comes, for then it will be too late to escape, the townspeople will certainly kill you."

Töltschig. "You forget that Gen. Oglethorpe promised us exemption from military service, and we claim the liberty he pledged."

Causton. "If the Count, and the Trustees and the King himself had agreed on that in London it would count for nothing here, if war comes it will be *fight or die.* If I were an officer on a march and met people who would not join me, I would shoot them with my own hand, and you can expect no other treatment from the officers here."

Töltschig. "We are all servants, and can not legally be impressed."

Causton. "If the Count himself were here he would have to take his gun on his shoulder, and all his servants with him. If he were living on his estate at Old Fort it would make no difference, for the order of the Magistrates must be obeyed. If the English, to whom the country belongs must fight, shall others go free?"

Töltschig finally yielded so far as to tell him the number of men in their company, "it could do no harm for we could be counted any day," but their names were resolutely withheld, and service firmly refused.

Then the townspeople took up the cry. Should they fight for these strangers who would not do their share toward defending the land? They would mob and kill them first! They only injured the colony at any rate, for they worked so cheaply that they lowered the scale of wages; and besides they received money from many people, for their services, but spent none because they made everything they needed for themselves!

Still the Moravians stood firm in their position, indeed they could do nothing else without stultifying themselves. The instructions from Zinzendorf and the leaders of the Church at Herrnhut, with the approval of the lot, were definite,—they should take no part in military affairs, but might pay any fines incurred by refusal. To Oglethorpe and to the Trustees they had explained their scruples, making freedom of conscience an essential consideration of their settling in Georgia, and from them they had received assurances that only freeholders were liable to military duty. Therefore they had claimed no land as individuals, but had been content to live, and labor, and be called "servants," paying each week for men to serve in the night watch, in place of the absent owners of the two town lots. In Savannah their views were well known, and to yield to orders from a Magistrate, who openly declared that promises made by the Trustees, who had put him in office, were not worth regarding, and who threatened them with mob violence, would have been to brand themselves as cowards, unworthy members of a Church which had outlived such dire persecution as that which overthrew the ancient Unitas Fratrum, and recreant to their own early faith, which had led them to abandon homes and kindred in Moravia, and seek liberty of conscience in another kingdom. That Georgia needed armed men to protect her from the Spaniards was true, but equally so she needed quiet courage, steady industry, strict honesty, and pious lives to develop her resources, keep peace with her Indian neighbors, and win the respect of the world, but these traits were hardly recognized as coin current by the frightened, jealous men who clamored against the Moravians.

On the 28th, it was demanded that the Moravians help haul wood to the fort which was being built. They replied that their wagon and oxen were at the officers' service without hire, and that they would feed the animals, but personally they could take no share in the work. This angered the people again, and several of the members began to wonder whether they might perhaps comply so far as to assist, as a matter of friendship, in hewing logs for the fort, refusing the wages paid to others. The lot was tried, and absolutely forbade it, which was well, for it developed that the people were watching for their answer, having agreed that if they helped on the fort it would be a proof that they *could* do what they chose, and were simply hiding behind an excuse in refusing to fight.

But the tension was not relaxed, and on the 2nd of March, the Moravians met to decide on their further course. Should they keep quiet, and wait for times to change, or should they go away? It was referred to the lot, and the paper drawn read *"go out from among them."* This meant not merely from the city, but from the province, for Mr. Causton had told them that they would be subject to the same requirements if they were living in the adjoining country.

On the strength of this they wrote a letter to Mr. Causton, rehearsing their motives in coming to Georgia, and the promises made them, reiterating their claim for liberty of conscience, and concluding, "But if this can not be allowed us, if our remaining here be burdensome to the people, as we already perceive it begins to be, we are willing, with the approbation of the Magistrate, to remove from this place; by this means any tumult that might ensue on our account will be avoided, and occasion of offense cut off from those who now reproach us that they are obliged to fight for us."

When it came to this point Mr. Causton found himself by no means anxious to drive away some thirty of his best settlers, who stood well with Oglethorpe and the Trustees, and had given him all their trade for supplies, so he began to temporize. "They trusted in God, and he really did not think their house would be burned over their heads." Töltschig said that was the least part of it, they had come for freedom, and now attempts were made to force them to act contrary to the dictates of their consciences. Then he declared that he had no power in the matter of their leaving, that must be settled between the Count, the Trustees, and themselves, but he could not permit them to go until he received an order from the Trustees. Meanwhile he would do what he could to quiet the people's dissatisfaction with them.

As their debt to the Trustees was not yet fully paid, Causton's refusal bound them in Savannah for the time being, according to their bond, so they had to turn elsewhere for help. Early in February, they had heard of Spangenberg's return to Pennsylvania from his visit to St. Thomas, and had written to ask him to come and help them for a while, but being busy with other things he did not go. On the 5th of March, Ingham suggested that he and one of their number should go to England to the Trustees. They thought it over and decided that George Neisser should go with him as far as Pennsylvania, where the case should be laid before Spangenberg, with the request that he go to London, arrange matters with the Trustees, and get permission for them to leave Georgia. Ingham was going, with the approval of Wesley and Delamotte, to try and bring over some of their friends to help in the work of evangelizing the Province.

A ship was ready to sail for Pennsylvania on the 9th, so Ingham and Neisser took passage on her, and sailed, as the event proved, never to return.

Chapter VI.

DISINTEGRATION.

Spangenberg's Visit.

After Spangenberg had decided not to comply with the request contained in the letter from Savannah, but to stay and prosecute the work among the Schwenkfelders, where a door seemed to be opening, he became conscious of a feeling of uneasiness, an impression that he was needed in Georgia. This was increased by news of the expected Spanish outbreak, for so general was the alarm that all the war-ships in the northern harbors were ordered to Carolina, and the selling of supplies to the Spaniards was absolutely prohibited.

At this point George Neisser and Benjamin Ingham came, bringing word of the pressure on the Moravians, their decision to leave Georgia as soon as it could be arranged, and their request that Spangenberg should go to England with Ingham to see the Trustees, and secure their consent. Of this plan Spangenberg did not approve, for he thought the war would ruin everything, or else the danger would be over, before he could make the long journey to England, and return. Ingham professed himself ready to carry letters to the Trustees, and do his best to influence them to grant the Moravian requests, so Spangenberg decided to entrust that errand to him, and himself go at once to Georgia, to see whether he could not help matters there.

John Eckstein, a resident of Germantown, a middle-aged man who was in entire sympathy with Spangenberg's plans for religous work in Pennsylvania, resolved to accompany him on his trip to Georgia. They sailed from Philadelphia on the 22nd of May, 1737, and had a long and very trying voyage. The Captain and crew were evil men, given to cursing and swearing, and more than once they threatened to murder the two passengers, whom they called sorcerers, and accused of bringing the continuous head winds and frequent storms upon them. Seventy-seven long days the voyage lasted; twice they sailed southward past Cape Hatteras, and twice were they driven back to north and east, taking weeks to recover the distance lost; and the Captain finally discovered that not only were the elements against him, but his helmsman was slyly hindering their progress all he could, for some malicious purpose of his own.

To the mental strain of the long journey was added physical discomfort, for firewood gave out, so that no cooking could be done, and for a month the crew lived on hard tack, dried cherries soaked in water, and raw fish,—dolphins caught as need required. Spangenberg and his companion had brought provisions to supplement the ship's fare, but long before the voyage was ended their store of butter and sugar was exhausted. Dried ham and tongue had a tendency to increase their thirst, but by soaking tea in cold water they made a beverage which bore at least a fancied resemblance to that brewed on shore. Then the supply of water ran low, each man's allowance was reduced to a pint a day, and even this small amount would have failed had they not been able occasionally to catch rain-water to replenish their casks. The Captain at last opened a keg of beer found in his cargo, and sold his passengers enough to relieve their thirst, for which they were very grateful.

But unkind words, delay, uncooked food, thirst, were not all that Spangenberg and his companion had to bear, for actual danger was added to their experience from time to time. High waves broke over the ship, winds tore away the sails, and a water-spout threatened total destruction. So late was the ship in reaching port that she was given up for lost, and word was sent to Pennsylvania which caused much grief,—needless grief, for Spangenberg's days of service were not to be ended thus. It sounds almost trivial to say that in the midst of trials of body, mind and soul Spangenberg occupied himself with making buttons, but no doubt the homely, useful labor did its part toward rendering endurable the seemingly endless days.

At last, on the 7th of August, the ship ran on a sandbank near Tybee, and the Moravians, hearing that Spangenberg was on board, took a boat and brought him to Savannah. They had asked him to go to England, he had disregarded their request and come to Georgia, but he was dear to them through many months of united service and mutual help, and they gave him a hearty welcome, ignoring all cause for complaint, and taking him at once into their full confidence. He and Töltschig sat up all of the first night carefully discussing the condition of affairs and what could be done to remedy them. Their views were very different, for Spangenberg thought they had been too hasty in deciding to leave Georgia, while Töltschig felt that it was a reflection on the lot to try and hold them in Savannah, when the lot had said "go." But Töltschig possessed the rare art of seeing a disputed question through the eyes of those who did not agree with him, as well as from his own standpoint, and now, with no petty self-assertion, he quietly awaited developments, and told Spangenberg all that had happened since Neisser's departure.

As the alarm concerning an immediate invasion by the Spanish had died away, the inhabitants of Savannah had regained their composure, and the wild outcry against the Moravians gradually ceased. The wagon and oxen which had been taken for work on the fort had been returned to their owners, after seven or eight weeks of hard usage, and the hope that starvation would shake the resolution of the non-combatants had signally failed of fulfillment. The ship which was to bring the town supplies had been twelve weeks late in coming, and the stock in the store-house was almost exhausted. The authorities therefore had announced that provisions would be sold only to those who were helping build the fort. This entirely excluded the Moravians, but instead of suffering from hunger they had been able to share with some of their neighbors. The prices charged at the store in Savannah were always high, so, as he was passing through New York on his return from St. Thomas, Spangenberg had asked a friend to send the Moravians two thousand pounds of flour and salt-meat, for which they were to pay. The merchant at that time knew of no ship sailing for Savannah, so in Philadelphia, Spangenberg had arranged that two thousand pounds of meat should be sent from there at once on a year's credit. Meanwhile the New York merchant found an opportunity to send what was ordered from him, so the Moravians had been surprised by a double quantity, which proved to be just what they needed during the general scarcity. When the friends in Pennsylvania heard that provisions had been sent, but not enough to last until the next harvest, they gave thirty-six hundred pounds of flour to Spangenberg to be taken, as a present, to the Georgia Moravians, and when word was received that Spangenberg's ship was lost, they sent an additional eighteen hundred pounds, so the "Society" was well supplied with this necessary article of food for some time to come.

In their household affairs the Moravians had had various experiences. Hermsdorf had been so thoroughly frightened by the demonstrations against the Moravians that on the 16th of May he had sailed for Germany, regardless of Töltschig's efforts to persuade him to wait, as his wife might even then be on her way to join him. Not only did he fear the townspeople so greatly that day and night he stayed in his room "as in a prison," but he was still more afraid to face Gen. Oglethorpe, who, it was said, would soon return. Only once had he joined in the devotional exercises of the household after his return from Frederica, and it was rather a relief when he left for home, having first repaid the amount of his passage to Georgia. He seems to have retained his connection with the Moravian Church, for he was in Herrnhut when Wesley visited there, and showed him many courtesies; and he is mentioned in 1742, as bearing letters to the "Sea Congregation," then about to sail for Pennsylvania.

On the 6th of June a four-year-old English boy had been taken into their household. He was an orphan, and they meant to bring him up, but the little fellow died on the 23rd of July.

On the 10th of June the matrimonial troubles of George Waschke and Juliana Jäschke had been happily terminated by their marriage. Waschke had been one of the discontents ever since the arrival of the second company, but when his marriage was finally arranged he professed himself contrite, and promised all obedience to the rules of the "Society," so long as he stayed in Savannah, though he retained his desire to leave as soon as possible. Juliana also had greatly improved in her behaviour before the wedding.

This marriage was the cause of a very interesting discussion among the Moravians, as to who should perform the ceremony. "In the afternoon the Brethren met to decide who should be appointed to marry Waschke and Juliana. Properly Br. Peter (Rose) should have been ordained by Br. Anton (Seifert) to the office of a "Diener" in the Congregation, that he might marry and baptize, but the Brethren did not think it necessary to ordain him on Waschke's account, and voted that Töltschig should marry them. He objected, but they said Töltschig had been made a 'Diener' of the Congregation at Herrnhut. He protested that he had not been sent to Georgia to marry and baptize, and did not wish to do it. The others insisted, and asked that the lot be tried; Töltschig agreed to submit to their wish, and the lot drawn read 'he shall marry these two,'" which he did the next day.

Parallel with this is the baptism of Rose's twin daughters, Anna Catherina and Maria Magdalena, who were born on the 16th of September, 1737,— Anna Catherina dying later in the same year. Of this Töltschig wrote: "I, at the request of the Brethren, baptized them in the name of the Father, the Son, and of the Holy Ghost, after Br. Anton (Seifert) had ordained me a "Diener" in the Congregation."

It frequently happens that a puzzling action becomes clear when it is considered from the standpoint of the man who has done it, but when the motive can not be fathomed many things are hard to understand. That Seifert had been empowered to delegate to another member a duty usually reserved for the clergy, was reasonable, though unusual, for his serious illness or death would have left the Congregation without ministration until word could be sent to Germany, and some one else could come to take his place,—a matter of months,—but, when the "Aeltester" was present, in full health, in entire accord with his Congregation, and when he in person confirmed candidates for Church membership, why did he not marry and baptize directly, instead of ordaining a "Diener" especially for those two offices? There must have been some regulation in the

Congregation at Herrnhut which led to it, for the idea that Seifert himself should marry Waschke and Juliana, and baptize the Rose children, evidently did not occur to them, but the rule can not now be found, and there is no clue to the strange proceeding.

Soon after the Waschke affair had been settled to the satisfaction of all parties, serious trouble had arisen with Jag and Haberecht. It was reported to the Moravians that Jag had engaged himself to a Swiss woman living in Savannah, and when questioned he admitted that it was true. They argued with him, and pled with him, but to no avail, and finally told him plainly that they would not allow him to bring the woman to their house, and more than that, if he persisted in his determination he would have to leave them; and angry and defiant he did take his departure the next day, July the 10th.

That "troubles never come singly" was exemplified, for the very day that Jag left, Haberecht went to Töltschig, and asked if some way could not be found so that *he* could marry that same Swiss woman! Töltschig was almost stunned by this second blow, and gave a stern answer, whereupon Haberecht applied to Seifert, the Aeltester, who was equally as unyielding in his condemnation of the acquaintance already made, and his refusal to countenance further steps. Poor Haberecht, less resolute than Jag in his rebellion, drank deeply of the waters of Marah during the next weeks; promising to give up the woman, who was really unworthy of his regard, and then trying to draw Töltschig into a discussion of his possible marriage; despairingly making his way to the garden to hide himself among the swine, feeling he was fit for no better company, and then going to the woman and asking her to marry him, to which she consented, having already thrown Jag over; again bitter repentance, confession, and a plea that his associates would forgive him. Either he was really in earnest this time, or Spangenberg's arrival had a salutary effect, for after that the Swiss woman disappears from the story, and two months later Jag returned, promised good behaviour, and humbly asked for readmittance to the household which was at once accorded him.

The first days of his visit to Savannah, Spangenberg spent in acquainting himself with the condition of affairs, and in interviews with the members singly and collectively, trying to persuade them to content themselves in Georgia. The "bands" were reorganized, but he was unable to re-establish a feeling of unity among them, and even those who were willing to stay, and work, and try whether their plan might not still be carried out, felt that it would be unwise to hold the rest, for as Töltschig wrote, almost with a groan, "it is a blessed thing to live with a little company of brethren, who are of one heart and one soul, where heart and mind are dedicated to Jesus, but so to live, when many have weak wills and principles, and there must be a community of goods, is rather difficult, especially when many seek their own ends, not the things of Christ."

Spangenberg was forced to see that his arguments were futile, and wisely yielded to the inevitable. At a general conference each man was called upon to state his wishes. Several desired to leave at the earliest possible moment, others as soon as the debt was fully paid; two or three wanted to return to Europe, others preferred to go to Pennsylvania to Spangenberg; some longed to live among the Indians as missionaries, while quite a number were content to stay in Savannah, unless absolutely forced to leave, or definitely called to labor elsewhere. However, no immediate steps were taken toward breaking up the settlement.

On the 12th of August, Spangenberg and Wesley visited the Salzburgers at Ebenezer, by the invitation of Bolzius, the senior pastor. They, too, had had their troubles without and within, and Gronau had mourned over the fact to the Moravians, who deeply sympathized with him. At this time Gronau and Bolzius differed greatly in their feeling for the Moravians. Gronau was openly and honestly on the best of terms with them, but Bolzius, while occasionally accepting their hospitality in Savannah, sent complaints to the Trustees, in keeping with his original protest against their coming to Georgia. The English friends of the Moravians heard of these letters, and were much puzzled, as the reports from the Savannah Congregation spoke only of pleasant relations with the Salzburgers, and requests for union of the two forces. Probably Bolzius was fretted by their refusal to join him, even as the leaders at Halle resented the independence of Herrnhut, and after Gronau's death, in 1745, the pastors of Ebenezer steadily opposed the efforts of the Moravians to recommence a mission work in Georgia.

Apart from the friction with their fellow townsmen and the lack of united purpose among their own number, Spangenberg found the Moravian colony in good condition. Their devotional hours were steadily observed, the Lord's Supper was celebrated regularly, and a weekly conference kept the many interests of the "Society" running smoothly.

By the aid of the second company, various improvements had been made, so that their lots and garden presented a prosperous appearance. "They have a house in town (on Spangenberg's lot) with a supply of wood for the kitchen. Behind the house is a well, with a pump, on which almost the whole town depends, for it not only never goes dry, as do all the others, but it has the best water to be found in the town. From early morning to late at night the people come with barrels, pails and pitchers, to take the water to their homes. Once some one suggested that strangers should be charged so much a pail for the benefit of the orphans, but Frank said 'they have so far received spiritual water from us without price, let them also have this freely.' Between the well and the house is a cow shed. They have a cow, which is pastured out during the day, but comes back in the evening, and they use the milk and butter for the sick. Near the shed is a kitchen and bake-oven, and on the other side a hut for their provisions. Behind the well, on Nitschmann's lot, stands on one side Tanneberger's and on the other Rose's cabin, with a roof between, under which the leather is stored, which is to be made into shoes.

"Two English miles from the town they have

cleared ten acres, (the garden) and planted corn and rice, which is growing nicely. They have set out mulberry, peach, and apple trees, which are doing well; in the middle of the garden, which is enclosed with a fence and ditch, they have built a corn-house, a cabin in which to live, and a stable." Another cabin, the first erected in the garden, had been burned in January, at which time Mrs. Waschke was living in it, though she was away when it caught fire, and returned too late to give an alarm and save it. The farm four miles from town was proving unsatisfactory, requiring much labor and yielding little return, and they had about decided to stop cultivating it, and give all their effort to the garden, which was paying well.

From the 14th to the 17th of August, Spangenberg busied himself with the account between the Moravians and the Trustees. In addition to the bonds signed by the first and second companies for their passage to Georgia, and provisions to be delivered on arrival, it had been necessary to get a great deal at the store on credit. On the other hand the men had done a considerable amount of carpenter work and hauling for the Trustees and for others. The account on the books at the Trustees' store was all in confusion, and as everybody at the store claimed to be too busy to unravel it, Spangenberg obtained permission to do it himself, and found that in addition to the bonds, (£60: and £226: 13: 9,) the Moravians had taken supplies to an amount which gave them a total debt of some £500: ($2,400.-00). Against this they had a credit which entirely paid their current account at the store, and reduced their debt to the Trustees to £121 : 2: 9, ($580.80).

On the 19th, a Lovefeast was held in honor of Spangenberg and Eckstein, and on the 21st of August the two visitors sailed for Pennsylvania, landing there safely in due time.

A CLOSING DOOR.

With the month of September letters began to come from England and Germany in response to Dober's report, and the communications sent by Ingham, who presented the Moravian request to the Trustees, (receiving "a sour answer,") and also sent a full account of their circumstances to Count Zinzendorf. The Count had already written to his distressed brethren, giving his advice on various points, and this letter, which was the first to arrive, gave them little comfort. They had once hoped for reinforcements, earnest men and women who would strengthen their hands for the work among the Indians, and even now it was disappointing to hear that Zinzendorf had decided not to send any more colonists to Georgia. He argued that it would take very few men to supply teachers for Tomochichi's little village, and that as the Trustees would only permit four missionaries among the more distant tribes, that number could easily be spared from the company already in Savannah.

Regarding military service he repeated his former definite instructions, "you will not bear arms either defensive or offensive." He said that he had tried to secure from the Trustees a formal "dispensation," either verbal or written, exempting the Moravians entirely from military duty, but they refused to give it, insisting that the Moravians must at least employ two men to represent the two town lots in defense of the country. Zinzendorf had agreed to this, so far as the night watch was concerned, since such a watch was necessary for civic peace and well-being, and the Moravians were authorized to pay the necessary sums therefor, but he considered it inconsistent to refuse to fight as a matter of conscience and then hire others to do it, and so, as he said, "there is nothing to do but to say *no,* and wait."

Although Spangenberg had hoped it would not be necessary for the Moravians to leave Georgia, he had sent the Trustees their request for permission to go, adding, "Nor indeed is there any reason why they should be detained, since it is their full intention and design to pay every farthing of their debt before they stir a foot; and they have never yet sold their liberty to any man, neither are they bound to any man by any writing or agreement whatsoever. I doubt not therefore but ye will readily shew the same clemency towards innocent and inoffensive men, which any one may expect from your Honors, whose business is not to destroy but to save and benefit mankind. May it please you therefore to send orders to the Magistrate of Savannah that these people may have leave to depart that Province. I do assure your Honors they always thought it a great favor that ye were pleased to send them thither; but now they will think it a greater to be dismissed."

In reply the Trustees wrote to Mr. Causton, forbidding the introduction of martial law without their express order, and reproving him for having required more than two men from the Moravians, but in that very reproof practically insisting that two must serve. The Moravians thought they had defined their position clearly at the outset, and believed they had the Trustees' promise that all should be as they desired, and if the Trustees realized the construction placed upon their words they had taken a most unfair advantage of the Moravians by offering them the two town lots as a special favor, and then using the ownership of those lots as a lever to force unwelcome service. On the other hand the Trustees claimed that Zinzendorf had tacitly agreed to furnish two fighting men when he allowed Spangenberg and Nitschmann to take the two freeholds, and one can hardly imagine that the gentlemen who served as Trustees of Georgia would stoop to a subterfuge to gain two soldiers. Probably it was an honest misunderstanding for which neither side was to blame, and of which neither could give a satisfactory explanation, each party having had a clear idea of his own position, and having failed to realize that in the confusion of tongues the other never did grasp the main point clearly.

Regarding the Moravian request for permission to leave, the Trustees declined to give instructions until after an exchange of letters with Zinzendorf; but in a second letter to his Congregation, the Count wrote, "If some do not wish to remain, let them go," and "if the authorities will not do what you demand it is certain that you must break up and go further; but whether to Pennsylvania, or New York or Carolina, the Lord will show you." Carolina would be no better than Georgia for their purpose, for the military conditions were identical, and Bishop Nitschmann's advice that they go to Pennsylvania, together with Spangenberg's residence there, decided them in favor of that location.

Zinzendorf's permission having cleared the way for departure, they resolved to wait no longer on the Trustees, and a general conference was held on September 18th, in which definite arrangements were made for the assumption of the debt by those who were willing as yet to remain in Georgia, freeing the four who were to go first. A recent letter had informed Tanneberger of the death of his wife and children in Herrnhut, and the news shattered his already weak allegiance. Without them he cared little where he went, or what became of him, if only he could get away, and Haberecht was more than ready to join him. His young son went as a matter of course, and Meyer, another member who had been lazy and unsatisfactory, completed the party, which sailed for Pennsylvania on the 16th of October. Jag also intended to go, but for some reason waited for the next company.

Haberecht settled at Ephrata, and the two Tannebergers at Germantown. In 1741, Haberecht joined the Moravians who were building in "the forks of the Delaware," and became one of the first members of the Bethlehem Congregation. In 1745, David Tanneberger married Regina Demuth, who had lost her husband the previous year, and they ultimately moved to Bethlehem also. Meyer never renewed his association with the Moravians.

Before the four started to Pennsylvania, another member had taken the longer journey, and had been laid beside his brethren in the Savannah cemetery. This was George Haberland, who died September 30th, from flux, a prevalent disease, from which almost all of the colonists suffered at one time or another. He had learned much during his life in Georgia, had been confirmed in June with his brother Michael, and had afterward served acceptably as a "Diener" of the Congregation.

On the 7th of October, Seifert and Böhner moved to Tomochichi's village to perfect themselves in the language, and begin their missionary work. As some of the congregation had already left Savannah, and others were soon to follow, Seifert thought that he could be spared even though he was "Aeltester," especially as at first he returned to Savannah every Saturday to hold the Sunday services. In November he and Böhner spent several weeks in town helping the carpenters raise the frame of a large house they were building, and when they returned to the Indians in January, 1738, Peter Rose, his wife, and surviving daughter went with them.

Friday, December 13th, John Wesley left Savannah, to return to England. His popularity had long since waned, in the face of his rigid insistence on ecclesiastical rules, and it was said "the Brethren alone can understand him, and remain in love with him." He was unfortunate enough to provoke a spiteful woman, a niece of Mr. Causton, the Magistrate, and so greatly did the persecution rage under her influence, that Wesley's chance of doing further good was ruined, and nothing was left but for him to withdraw. The Magistrates forbade him to leave, (secretly rejoicing that they had driven him away,) but he boldly took his departure, without molestation, making his way to Beaufort, where Charles Delamotte joined him. Together they went to Charlestown, where he parted from Delamotte, and on the 2nd of January, 1738, sailed from the continent that had witnessed the shattering of so many fond hopes and ambitions.

Forty-seven years later Brierly Allen settled in Savannah, the first minister there to represent the great denomination which grew from Wesley's later work in England, and the first Methodist Society in that city of his humiliation was organized in 1806.

During the preceding summer Zinzendorf had written to the Trustees, asking once more for (1) entire exemption from military service for the Georgia Moravians, for (2) permission for them to leave Georgia if this could not be granted, and (3) that at least four might remain among the Indians as missionaries.

In answer the Trustees (1) repeated their former decision regarding freehold representation, (2) gave consent for the Moravians to leave if they would not comply with this, and (3) refused to let them stay as missionaries. "The privilege of going among the Indians was given to your people out of consideration for Your Excellency, and also on account of their good conduct, they being citizens of this colony; but if they cease to reside there, this privilege will not be continued to any of them. To employ them as missionaries to instruct the Indians would be a reflection on our country, as if it could not furnish a sufficient number of pious men to preach the Gospel of Jesus Christ. Therefore your people may continue among the Indians, only so long as they are citizens of the colony."

This was the death-blow to the Moravian settlement in Georgia. Had the Trustees exemplified their much-vaunted religious toleration by respecting the conscientious scruples of the Moravians, there were enough members of the Savannah Congregation who wanted to stay in Georgia to form the nucleus of the larger colony which would surely have followed them, for while they were willing to give up everything except religious liberty, they were human enough to regret having to abandon the improvements which they had made at the cost of so much labor and self-denial. The Church at large shared this feeling, and for many years watched and waited for an opportunity to re-open the work in Savannah, but without result. If the Trustees had even permitted the Moravians to stay as missionaries it might have saved the settlement to Georgia, for within a decade the English Parliament passed an Act granting the Moravians the very exemption for which they now asked in vain, and had there been a promising work begun among the Indians during the intervening years it would inevitably have drawn more laborers, as it did in Pennsylvania. But the Trustees shut the door in their faces, other promising and more hospitable fields opened, and the Moravian efforts were thereafter given to the upbuilding of other commonwealths.

In the latter part of January, 1738, eight more of the Moravian colonists left Savannah,—Gotthard

Demuth and his wife, George Waschke, his wife and mother, Augustin Neisser, Gottlieb Demuth, and David Jag, those who remained giving them money and provisions for their journey to Pennsylvania. Gotthard Demuth and wife settled in Germantown, later moving to Bethlehem and joining in the organization of that Congregation. In 1743 they were again living at Germantown, where Gotthard died the following year. Regina subsequently married David Tanneberger and moved once more to Bethlehem. Gottlieb Demuth lived at several places, but finally married, and settled in the Moravian Congregation at Schoeneck. Jag, who located at Goshenhopper, and the Waschkes and Augustin Neisser who went to Germantown, never rejoined the Church.

On the 28th of January, the Moravians in Savannah received an unlooked-for addition to their number. Töltschig wrote to Spangenberg, "Yesterday two boys, who belong to Herrnhut, came unexpectedly to our house. They ran away from the Brethren in Ysselstein and went to Mr. Oglethorpe in London, begging him to send them to the Brethren in Georgia. He did so, but we will have to pay their transportation. One is Zeisberger's son David, about 17 years old, and the other John Michael Schober, about 15 years old. Both are bad boys." It appears that when Zeisberger's parents went to Georgia he was left in Herrnhut to finish his education. From there Count Zinzendorf took him to a Moravian settlement near Utrecht, Holland, where he was employed as errand boy in a shop. He was treated with well-meant but ill-judged severity, and finally after a particularly trying and undeserved piece of harshness in October, 1737, he and his friend Schober decided to try and make their way to his parents in Georgia. In this they succeeded, and though their story was received with disapprobation, they soon made a place for themselves. Schober did not live very long, but Zeisberger, from the "bad boy" of Töltschig's letter, became the assistant of Peter Böhler in South Carolina, and later the great "apostle to the Indians."

During this Spring the Moravians strained every nerve to do an amount of work sufficient to balance their account with the Trustees. It took a little longer than they expected, but at last Töltschig was ready for his journey to England, the lot having previously decided that he should go as soon as financial affairs made it proper. His wife remained in Savannah, it being uncertain whether he would stay in Germany or return to America. John Regnier took his place as financial agent of the Moravians.

On March 12th, Töltschig went aboard a ship, bound for Charlestown, sailing from Tybee two days later. On the 18th, he reached Charlestown, whence he sailed April 1st, bearing with him the record of their account with the Trustees, and commissioned to tell the authorities at Herrnhut all about the Georgia colony. On the 30th of May, the vessel touched at Cowes, where Töltschig landed, making his way overland to London which he reached on the 2nd of June.

On the 11th of June, Töltschig, accompanied by

Richter, went to present the account to the Trustees. They asked him many questions concerning Georgia, all of which he answered frankly, receiving most courteous attention. Three days later a settlement was reached. The written accounts showed that the Moravians were short £3 : 5 : 5, which Töltschig offered to pay in cash, but the Trustees said they realized that the supplies provided for in the second bond had been rated at a higher price in Georgia than in England, and they were content to consider the obligations as fully discharged, interest included. Töltschig answered "I am *very* glad," a short sentence which spoke volumes!

WESLEY, INGHAM AND TÖLTSCHIG.

During the days which elapsed between his arrival in London and the meeting of the Trustees, Töltschig had many interviews with those who had been "awakened" by the two companies of Moravian colonists, by Count Zinzendorf, and by Peter Böhler and George Schulius. The last two were even then at Portsmouth, on their way to America, and the interest caused by their visit was very manifest.

John and Charles Wesley had been particularly attracted to Böhler, the former especially finding great relief in laying his many spiritual perplexities before him. Wesley complained that when he conversed with Spangenberg in Georgia, and they could not agree on any point, Spangenberg would drop the subject and refuse to discuss it further, but in Böhler he found a clearness of argument, and power of persuasion which convinced without irritating him.

PETER BOEHLER.

Having passed through many stages with the guidance, sympathy and encouragement of Böhler, Wesley at last found the assurance of salvation he had sought for so many years, and three weeks after Böhler left London, he records that at a meeting of their society "I felt I did trust in Christ, Christ alone for salvation, and an assurance was given me that he had taken away my sins, even mine, and saved me from the law of sin and death." A few days previously his brother Charles had made the same happy experience, and this gave to their religious life the warmth and fervor which, added to the zeal, industry and enthusiasm that had always characterized them, made their labors of so much value to England, and founded the denomination which has grown so rapidly in America, still bearing the name once given in derision to the little group of Oxford "Methodists."

But Wesley's mind was not one of those which can rest contentedly upon one vital truth, he must needs run the whole gamut of emotion, and resolve every point raised by himself or others into a definite negative or affirmative in his own life. Once settled in a position to his entire satisfaction, he was as immovable as a mountain, and this was at once the source of his power and his weakness, for thousands gladly followed the resolute man, and found their own salvation therein, while on the other hand the will which would never bend clashed hopelessly with those who wished sometimes to take their turn in leading. So he became an outcast from the Church of England, alienated from Ingham, Whitefield, and other friends of his youth, estranged from the Moravians, even while he was one of the greatest religious leaders England has ever produced.

At the time of Töltschig's sojourn in London, however, he was in the early, troubled stage of his experience, rejoicing in what he had attained through Böhler's influence, but beset with doubts and fears. And so, as he records in his Journal, he determined "to retire for a short time into Germany, where he hoped the conversing with those holy men who were themselves living witnesses of the full power of faith, and yet able to bear with those that are weak, would be a means, under God, of so establishing his soul, that he might go on from faith to faith, and from strength to strength."

Ingham, meanwhile, informed of Töltschig's arrival in London, had hastened "over one hundred and forty miles" to see his friend, a fact that seems to have touched Töltschig deeply, and arranged to go with him to Herrnhut, as they had often planned while still in Georgia. John Wesley joined them, and the three young men sailed on June 24th, landing at Rotterdam two days later. Wesley's Journal does not mention Töltschig by name, but on leaving Rotterdam he says, "we were eight in all, five English and three Germans," and there is no doubt that Töltschig went with them to Marienborn to report to Count Zinzendorf, who was living there during his temporary exile from Herrnhut.

In Rotterdam, Dr. Koker showed the party much kindness, while at Baron von Watteville's in Ysselstein, they were received "as at home." At Amsterdam, they joined in the meeting of the "societies" established under Moravian influences, and from there proceeded to Cologne, and up the Rhine to Frankfort. Having neglected to supply themselves with passports, they experienced much difficulty whenever they reached a walled city, sometimes being refused admittance altogether, and at other times being allowed to enter only after much delay, which caused Wesley to "greatly wonder that common sense and common humanity do not put an end to this senseless, inhuman usage of strangers." When any of their number had an acquaintance in the city to which they had come they sent in a note to him, and he would arrange for their entrance, and at Frankfort they applied to Peter Böhler's father, who entertained them "in the most friendly manner."

On Tuesday, July 15th, they reached Marienborn, where Wesley remained for fifteen days, and Ingham for about seven weeks.

From Marienborn, Wesley went to Herrnhut, stopping at Erfurt, Weimar, Jena, Halle, Leipsig and Dresden on the way. He remained at Herrnhut twelve days, and then returned by the same route to Marienborn, and to England.

This trip to Germany has been given as the beginning of the breach between Wesley and the Moravians, but it is doubtful whether such was really the case. In the "Memoirs of James Hutton" it is stated that Wesley was offended because Ingham was admitted to the Communion at Marienborn, while permission was refused him, and that he secretly brooded over the injury, but Wesley himself does not mention the occurrence, and refers to Marienborn as a place where he met what he "sought for, viz.: living proofs of the power of faith," and where he stayed twelve days longer than he at first intended. The tone of his account of Herrnhut is also distinctly friendly, though he did not unreservedly accept two or three theological statements made to him, but the long conversations he records prove his joy at finding sympathy, and confirmation of what he wanted to believe concerning justification by faith, and the fact that a weak faith was still a real faith, and as such should be cherished and strengthened, not despised. He could not have been greatly influenced against the Moravians by his visit to Halle, for each time he stayed but one night, and on the first occasion Professor Francke was not at home, nor were their arguments new to him, that they should have impressed him deeply.

It frequently happens that when a controversy has arisen between friends, both parties look backward and read into former words and deeds a meaning they did not have at the time they transpired, and most probably this is what has happened in regard to the trip to Germany and its effect on Wesley.

Immediately on his return to England, Wesley began an active religious campaign, drawing such crowds of all kinds of people that the various churches in turn closed their doors upon him, and eight months later he followed Whitefield into open air preaching, after consultation with the Fetter Lane Society. This Society had been organized at the time of Böhler's visit to London, and was composed of members of the earlier Methodist societies,

Germans residing in London, and English who had been interested in salvation by Zinzendorf and the Moravian companies bound for Georgia. It had met in the home of James Hutton until it outgrew the rooms, and was then transferred to the Chapel at 32 Fetter Lane. It was an independent Society, with no organic connection with the Moravian Church, and the religious work was carried on under the leadership of John Wesley, and, in his frequent absences, by James Hutton and others who leaned strongly toward the Moravians, some of whose customs had been adopted by the Society. The Hutton "Memoirs" state that Wesley made an effort to break off intercourse between the Society and the Moravians soon after his return from Germany, but failed, and matters continued to move smoothly until about the time that Wesley began his field preaching. During the subsequent months disputes arose among the members, largely on account of views introduced by Philip Henry Molther, who at that time had a tendency toward "Quietism." Molther was detained for some time in England, waiting for a ship to take him to Pennsylvania, he having received a call to labor in the Moravian Churches there, and being a fluent speaker he learned English rapidly and made a deep impression on many hearers.

Wesley was much hurt by the dissensions in his Society, and entirely opposed to Molther's views, and after several efforts to bring all the members back to his own position, he, on Sunday, July 31st, 1740, solemnly and definitely condemned the "errors" and withdrew from the Fetter Lane Society, adding "You that are of the same judgment, follow me." About twenty-five of the men and "seven or eight and forty likewise of the fifty women that were in the band" accepted his invitation, and with them he organized the "Foundry Society." Into the Foundry Society and the many others organized among his converts, Wesley introduced lovefeasts and "bands" (or "classes,") both familiar to him from the Fetter Lane Society, which had copied them from the Moravians. When his societies grew so numerous that he could not personally serve them all he selected lay assistants, and then "became convinced that presbyter and bishop are of the same order, and that he had as good a right to ordain as to administer the Sacraments." He, therefore, ordained bishops for America, and Scotland, and registered his chapels in order to protect them, according to the Act of Toleration. This gave the Methodist body a separate legal status, but Wesley always claimed that he was still a member of the Church of England, and would not allow the preachers of his English societies to administer the Sacraments, a right which was finally granted them by the Methodist Conference after his death.

When Benjamin Ingham returned from Georgia he commenced to preach the Gospel in Yorkshire, his native place, and at the time of his journey to Germany a promising work was begun there. From Herrnhut he wrote to Count Zinzendorf asking that Töltschig be permitted to visit him in England, and the request was granted a few months later. Meanwhile Ingham's work prospered mightily, so that in June, 1739, he was forbidden the use of the churches, and forced to imitate Wesley and preach in the open air. Some forty societies were formed, and in November, Töltschig went to him, making many friends among the people, repeating his visit at intervals during the following months.

The intimacy between Ingham and the Moravians became closer and closer, and in July, 1742, he formally handed over the care of his societies in Yorkshire and Lascashire to the Moravian Church, himself going into new fields, and then giving new societies into their keeping. It has often been stated that Ingham was a Moravian, but this is a mistake. During these years he worked with them shoulder to shoulder, but there is no record of his having been received into their Church as a member, nor did they reordain him into their ministry. The situation would be more strange to-day than it was then, for there was apparent chaos in England, the Spirit of God moving upon the face of the waters before "light shone, and order from disorder sprung," and the Moravians did not care to emphasize their independence of the Anglican Church lest it injure their usefulness. In 1744, when England was threatened with a French invasion, a number of loyal addresses were presented to the King, and among them one from the "United Brethren in England, in union with the ancient Protestant Episcopal Bohemian and Moravian church," a designation selected after long and careful discussion as to a true term which would avoid placing them among the Dissenters from the Church of England.

When the Moravians took over the Yorkshire Societies in 1742 they established headquarters at Smith House, near Halifax, but this not proving permanently available, Ingham, in 1744, bought an estate near Pudsey, where the Moravians planted a settlement which they called "Lamb's Hill," later "Fulneck." In 1746 and 1749 Ingham presented to the Moravians the ground on which the Chapel and two other houses stood, but for the rest they paid him an annual rent. The property is now held of Ingham's descendents on a lease for five hundred years.

In 1753 Ingham withdrew from his close association with the Moravians, and established a new circle of societies, himself ordaining the ministers who served them. These societies flourished for a while, but about 1759 Ingham became imbued with the doctrines of a certain Sandeman, and the result was the almost total wrecking of his societies. This broke Ingham's heart, and affected his mind, so that his last days were very sad. He passed away in 1772, and his societies gradually merged themselves into other churches.

John Töltschig, Ingham's friend in Georgia and his co-laborer in Yorkshire, came to England in November, 1739, in company with Hutton, who had been to Germany to form a closer acquaintance with the Moravians. After the debt to the Trustees was paid, Töltschig had eagerly planned new things for Georgia,—extension of work among the Indians, a settlement further up the Savannah River, the strengthening of the Savannah Congregation, from which missionaries could be drawn and by which they should be supported while laboring among the heathen tribes. He offered to return to America at once, ready for any duty, but requesting that he might not be sole financial manager again, as he had found it most difficult to attend to those duties, and at the same time share in the spiritual work.

The elders of the Church, after carefully weighing all the circumstances, decided not to send him back to Georgia, but that he should go to England, to labor in the Fetter Lane Society, and among its friends.

The first step was a visit to Ingham in Yorkshire, and the reception given him was so cordial and the field so promising that he went again, and yet again. Böhler and Spangenberg returned to England and traveled hither and thither in response to the calls that came from every side, other members aided as they could, and the societies under their direction grew apace. Fetter Lane Society was organized into a congregation in November, 1742, and the others followed in due time. The Moravian Church was introduced into Ireland, and took a firm hold there. In England its successes were paralleled with much opposition, and in 1749, after several years of preparation, an appeal was made to Parliament for recognition as a Protestant Episcopal Church, with full liberty of conscience and worship throughout Great Britain and her colonies. General Oglethorpe warmly championed their cause, and after a thorough investigation of Moravian history and doctrine, the bill was passed, May 12th, 1749, and the Moravian right to liberty of worship, freedom from military service, and exemption from oath-taking was unreservedly granted.

While not involved in these Parliamentary proceedings, Töltschig played an important part in the development of the Moravian Church in England and Ireland. Although he had great success as a preacher, his especial talents were as an organizer, and as leader of the "bands," as might be expected of a man with a judicial mind, executive ability, and great tact. He was Elder of the "Pilgrim Congregation" formed at Fetter Lane in May, 1742, a congregation composed exclusively of "laborers" in the Lord's vineyard, and he was also one of the committee charged with the oversight of the general work.

In February, 1748, he went to Ireland, as superintendent of the societies there, some of which had been organized by Wesley, but now wished to unite with the Moravians. In 1752 he conducted a company of colonists to Pennsylvania, but the next year went back to Ireland, where certain troubles had arisen which he could quiet better than any one else.

After Zinzendorf's death in 1760, Töltschig was one of that company of leading men who met in Herrnhut to provide for the immediate needs of the Moravian Church, whose enemies prophesied disintegration upon the death of the man who had been at its head for more than thirty years. These predictions failed of fulfillment, and "it was demonstrated that the Lord had further employment for the Unitas Fratrum."

Less renowned than many of his confreres, Töltschig was a type of that class of Moravians who carried their Church through slight and blight into the respect and good-will of the world. Industrious and scrupulously exact in business affairs, courteous and considerate in his dealings with others, firm and fearless in matters of conscience, bold to declare his faith, and witness for his Master, energetic and "conservatively progressive" in promoting the growth of his church, he took little part in the controversies of his day, but devoted himself unreservedly to preaching the Gospel as it was read by John Hus, by the founders of the ancient Unitas Fratrum, by the renewers of that Church in Herrnhut, "Salvation by faith in Christ and real Christian living according to the precepts of the Bible."

THE NEGRO MISSION.

John Töltschig had been the diarist of the Moravian Congregation in Savannah, as well as their treasurer and most able member, and after he left very little record was kept of the daily occurrences. A few stray letters have been preserved, but little of interest appears therein, beyond the facts that the summer of 1738 was hot and dry, and that the Moravians were not molested, although always conscious of the under-current of antagonism.

Some time during these months Matthias Seybold left for Pennsylvania, where he married, and was one of the company that established the settlement at Bethlehem. He returned to Europe in 1742, and died at Herrnhut in 1787.

In May, the Rev. George Whitefield reached Georgia, "authorized to perform all religious offices as Deacon of the Church of England, in Savannah and Frederica," in the place of John Wesley. The poverty of the people touched him deeply, he distributed to the most needy such sums as he had brought for their relief, and with James Habersham, who had come over at the same time, he agreed upon the erection of an Orphan House. Whitefield visited Ebenezer, and acquainted himself with conditions there and elsewhere, and then returned to England, in August, to raise funds for his Orphan House, Habersham meanwhile beginning to collect and instruct the most neglected children.

During his stay in Georgia, Whitefield lodged with Charles Delamotte, who was still carrying on the little school. During the winter Delamotte had boarded for a while with the Moravians, and when he returned to England in the autumn, he at once associated himself with the English members. Tyerman in his "Life and Times of John Wesley," says, "On his return to England, Charles Delamotte became a Moravian, settled at Barrow-upon-Humber, where he spent a long life of piety and peace, and died in 1790."

On the 16th of October, Peter Böhler and George Schulius arrived in Savannah, accompanied by the lad, Simon Peter Harper. They came as missionaries to the negroes of Carolina, the hearts of various philanthropic Englishmen having been touched by reports of the condition of these half wild savages recently imported from the shores of Africa to till the fields of the New World.

The plan originated during Count Zinzendorf's visit to London, in February, 1737, when it was suggested to him that such a mission should be begun by two Moravian men, under the auspices of "the associates of the late Dr. Bray."

Thomas Bray, an English divine, was born in 1656, made several missionary trips to America, and in 1697 organized a society for the propagation of the Gospel in the English Colonies. He died in 1730, but the work was continued by his "associates," many of whom were also interested in the Georgia Colony.

As this mission was to be under their direction, "the associates of the late Dr. Bray" wished to be very sure that the doctrine and rules of the Unitas Fratrum did not conflict with the Church of England, but being assured by the Archbishop of Canterbury that he considered them as agreeing in all essential points, they closed an agreement with Zinzendorf whereby the Count received £30: with which to prepare "two Brethren to reside for the instruction of the Negroes at such place in Carolina as the said associates shall direct." The missionaries, when they had entered upon their work, were to receive a salary, "not exceeding thirty pounds a year," from the "associates."

For this missionary enterprise, so much to his liking, Zinzendorf appointed "one of my chaplains, master Böhler," and "Schulius, a Moravian brother," who with Richter and Wenzel Neisser arrived in London, February 18th, 1738. At the house of their friend Wynantz, the Dutch merchant, they met John Wesley, who offered to secure them a pleasant, inexpensive lodging near James Hutton's, where he was staying.

Peter Böhler had been a student at Jena when Spangenberg was lecturing there, and was himself a professor at that seat of learning when he decided to accept Zinzendorf's call to mission work, and join the Moravians, with whom he had been for a long time in sympathy. Like Spangenberg he was a highly educated man, and an able leader, fitted to play an important part in the Church of his adoption. In December, 1737, he was ordained at Herrnhut by the bishops, David Nitschmann and Count Zinzendorf, and in later years he, too, became a bishop of the Unity.

On the 22nd of February, Böhler and his companions called on Gen. Oglethorpe, who at first supposed they were simply going over to join the Savannah congregation. Böhler explained that Richter, who spoke French as well as German, had come as the Agent of the Moravians, in accordance with the suggestion made by the Trustees to Bishop Nitschmann in 1736; that Wenzel Neisser was going on an official visitation to America, especially to the West Indies; and that he and Schulius were the missionaries promised by Count Zinzendorf for work among the negroes in Carolina. The General courteously invited them to confer with him further, either by letter or in person, and offered to take them with him, as he expected shortly to sail for Georgia with his regiment.

Later, when they wished to come to a definite agreement with Oglethorpe, who represented the "associates of Dr. Bray," they experienced some difficulty, owing to the fact that a letter of introduction Oglethorpe expected to receive from Count Zinzendorf had failed to arrive, but the exhibition of their passports, and Richter's explanation that Zinzendorf thought (from newspaper notices) that

Oglethorpe had already left England, enabled Böhler and Schulius to establish their identity. So soon as Zinzendorf heard that his word was needed, he sent them a formal letter of introducton to Oglethorpe, which was gladly received as corroboration of their statements. The Moravians were at their own expense while waiting in London, but Oglethorpe promised that they should be provided with Bibles, grammars, and other things they might need for the negro school.

Being detained in London for three months, instead of three weeks as they expected, Böhler and his friend had ample opportunity to make acquaintances in the metropolis. They sent word of their arrival to those Germans who had learned to know Zinzendorf and the earlier Moravian emigrants to Georgia, and on the first Sunday "the brethren," (as they affectionately called all who, like themselves, were interested in living a Christian life,) came to them, and a series of meetings for prayer, conference, and instruction was begun. Böhler was a man of attractive personality, and convincing earnestness, and in spite of his slight knowledge of their language many English also became interested and formed a society similar to that begun by Zinzendorf, the two soon uniting in the Fetter Lane Society.

Ten days after Böhler reached London he accepted an invitation from the two Wesleys, and went with them to Oxford. There he was most kindly received, preached in Latin once or twice each day, and had many private conversations with inquirers.

Among those with whom he became acquainted was the Rev. John Gambold, who later became a bishop in the Moravian Church, and many others were mightily stirred to seek the salvation of their souls.

Noting how little English Böhler and Schulius knew, Gen. Oglethorpe offered them a boy who was bright and intelligent, could speak both English and German, and understood some French, and they found him so serviceable that they asked and obtained permission to take him with them to Carolina.

Through Wesley, Böhler heard that Gen. Oglethorpe was much surprised at the speed with which he acquired English, and that he had asked whether Böhler would consent to serve as Minister of the Church of England in Savannah, if that Congregation remained without a pastor. Böhler expressed his willingness to preach at any time, but declined to administer the Sacraments for any denomination except his own, so the appointment was not made.

On the 28th of April, the baggage of the Missionaries was put aboard the *Union Galley,* Capt. Moberley, with instructions that Böhler and his companions should join her at Portsmouth. Neisser was to go with them to Georgia, and from there, as opportunity offered, to St. Thomas, but while the ship lay at Portsmouth other instructions reached him, and Oglethorpe kindly made no objection to his withdrawing his box and staying behind, though he did not quite understand it.

On the 15th of May, Peter Böhler, George Schulius, and the lad Simon Peter Harper, left London, but finding the ship not yet ready to sail, they, by Oglethorpe's instructions, went to Southampton where some of the vessels were lying.

Returning to Portsmouth they embarked on May 22nd, and soon found they were "to dwell in Sodom and Gomorrah" during their voyage. On the 30th the fleet sailed to Southampton for the soldiers, and when they came aboard four days later "Sodom and Gomorrah were fully reproduced." As the ships lay off Spithead a conspiracy was discovered,—the soldiers on one vessel had planned to kill their officers, take what money they could find, and escape to France. During the voyage there were several fights among the soldiers, or between them and the sailors, and in one drunken riot a soldier cut off a young girl's hand. "The Lord was our defense and shield, and we were among them like Daniel in the midst of the lions," wrote Böhler, for the quiet, Bible-reading Moravians found little to like in their rough associates, who cared for them just as little, and wished they could be thrown overboard.

The ships put to sea July 16th and reached the Madeiras on the 29th, where they were detained until the 8th of August. Böhler and Schulius went on shore a number of times, were courteously treated by the most prominent Catholic priest there, climbed a mountain for the exercise, and particularly enjoyed their escape from turmoil and confusion. The captain, who had taken a dislike to them, tried to prevent their leaving the ship, but Oglethorpe stood their friend, and ordered that they should have entire liberty. For Böhler, as for many who had preceded him, Georgia and Carolina were to be a school where great life lessons would be learned. Fresh from the

University halls of Jena, he had met the students of Oxford on equal footing, quickly winning their respect and admiration, but these soldiers and sailors, restless, eager for excitement, rude and unlettered, were a new thing to him, a book written in a language to which he had no key. Later he would learn to find some point of contact with the unlearned as well as the learned, with the negro slave and the Yorkshire collier as well as the student of theology, but just now his impulse was to hold himself aloof and let their wild spirits dash against him like waves about the base of a lighthouse which sends a clear, strong beam across the deep, but has few rays for the tossing billows just beneath.

On the 18th of September land was sighted, and on the 29th the fleet anchored in the harbor of St. Simon's Island, and with grateful hearts the Moravians watched the landing of the soldiers. On the 4th of October they transferred their baggage to a sloop bound for Savannah, which sailed the 6th, but on account of head winds did not reach Savannah until the 16th. The Moravians still at Savannah came in a boat to welcome them, and take them to their house, but Böhler was anxious to see the scene of his future labors, and stayed in town only a few days, leaving on the 21st for a tour through Carolina. Schulius accompanied him all the way, and several others as far as the Indian town where Rose was living with his wife and child. Here they talked of many things regarding the Savannah Congregation, but on the following afternoon the missionaries went on their way, Zeisberger, Haberland, Böhner and Regnier accompanying them to Purisburg.

There Böhler and Schulius lodged with one of the Swiss who had come to Georgia with Spangenberg and the first company. His wife expressed the wish that the Moravians in Savannah would take her thirteen-year-old daughter the following winter, and give her instruction, for which she would gladly pay. Böhler took occasion to speak to the couple about salvation and the Saviour, and they appeared to be moved. Indeed this was the main theme of all his conversations. To the owners of the plantations visited, he spoke of their personal needs, and their responsibility for the souls of their slaves; while to the slaves he told the love of God, filling them with wonder, for most of them were newly imported from the wilds of Africa, and suspicious even of kindness, many knew little of the English tongue, and the few who could understand his words had not yet learned that there was a God who cared how they lived or what became of them. Their masters, as a rule, thought the missionaries were attempting an almost hopeless task in trying to lift these negroes above the brute creation, but were quite willing to give permission and an opportunity to reach them, and on this tour Böhler found only one land-owner who refused his consent.

Purisburg had been named as the location of the negro school, but Böhler found there were very few negroes in the town, which had been largely settled by Swiss, who had not prospered greatly and had bought few slaves. The nearest plantation employing negroes was five miles distant, and only seven lived there, so the outlook was far from encouraging at that point.

Böhler and Schulius then made their way from one plantation to another, until they reached Charlestown. The Rev. Mr. Garden, to whom they had a letter of introduction, advised that the school should be begun in Charlestown, where there was a large negro population, perhaps a thousand souls. This was more than could be found on any single plantation in Carolina, and as the slaves were strictly forbidden to go from one plantation to another it would hardly be possible to find another place where so many could be reached at the same time. Böhler and Schulius were much impressed with the advantages offered, especially as Mr. Garden promised all the assistance he could give, and they debated whether Schulius should not stay and begin at once, while Böhler returned to report to Oglethorpe. The lot was finally tried, and the direction received that they should carefully study the situation but wait until later to commence work. Therefore on the 1st of November the two companions set out for Savannah, which they reached in eight days.

The following weeks were a sore trial for the missionaries. With a promising field in sight, and eager to commence work in it, they were obliged to wait for Oglethorpe's permission, and Oglethorpe was very busy on the frontier establishing the outposts for which his regiment had been brought over. When he did return to Savannah, it was only for a few hours, and he was in no frame of mind for a long argument of pros and cons. He told Böhler rather testily that they should not go to Charlestown with his consent; that if they were not willing to follow the plan for Purisburg he would have nothing more to do with them; and that if they wanted to talk further they must wait till he came again.

Böhler and Schulius wished themselves free to proceed without his consent, wished they had not entered into an agreement with "the associates of the late Dr. Bray," but under the circumstances felt themselves bound to give the work at Purisburg a fair trial. In December, Schulius went to Purisburg to look over the field, and make acquaintance with the people, while Böhler waited at Savannah for Oglethorpe, and finally, when his patience was quite exhausted, followed the General to St. Simons. Oglethorpe persisted in his intention to have the school at Purisburg, and when he learned that his wishes would be obeyed he gave instructions for the renting of a large house and two acres of ground, and for supplies to be furnished from the store at Savannah.

In February, 1739, therefore, Böhler and Schulius settled in Purisburg. Young Harper seems to have been with them in Purisburg on some of their earlier visits, but was sent temporarily to Savannah, and as he does not reappear in the records, he probably went back to his English home. David Zeisberger, Jr., joined Böhler and was his willing helper in many ways.

At first the outlook was rather more promising than they expected. There were very few colored children for the school, but "daily more were bought and born," there was some interest aroused among the older negroes, and the owners were disposed to be friendly, and allow the missionaries free access to their slaves. The German and Swiss settlers were unaffectedly glad to have the Moravians in their midst, and begged for religious services, and instruction for their children, so Böhler and Schulius agreed on a division of labor, the latter to devote himself to the white residents and their little ones, while Böhler spent most of his time visiting adjoining plantations.

But when the warm weather came Böhler was taken with fever, and from June to October he suffered severely. From time to time he was able to be up, and even to visit Savannah, but he was so weak and his feet were so badly swollen that walking was very difficult, and of course missionary tours were impossible.

On the 4th of August, George Schulius died, after an illness of eighteen days' duration. Böhler was in Savannah when he was taken sick, but returned in time to nurse him, to soothe him in delirium, and to lay him to rest amid the lamentations of the Purisburg residents. At his death the school for white children was given up, for Böhler was too weak to shoulder the additional load, and felt that his first duty was to the negroes. In September, Oglethorpe was in Savannah, and after much difficulty Böhler obtained speech with him, and succeeded in convincing him that a negro school at Purisburg was hopeless. He approved of Böhler's plan to itinerate among the plantations and promised that both his own and Schulius' salaries should be paid him, that he might be supplied for traveling expenses. In November, when his health was restored, Böhler wished to make his first journey, but the storekeeper declined to pay him any money until the expiration of the quarter year. When he went again at the appointed time the storekeeper refused to pay anything without a new order from Oglethorpe, except the remainder of the first year's salary, now long overdue. Böhler concluded that the man had received private instructions from Oglethorpe, and that his services were no longer desired by the representative of "the associates," so in January, 1740, he gave up further thought of obligation to them, and prepared to go on his own account. He planned to go by boat to Purisburg and from there on foot through Carolina to Charlestown, but on the way up the Savannah River the canoe was overtaken by a severe thunder storm, and forced to land. Knowing that a sloop would sail in two days he returned to Savannah, meaning to go to Charlestown on her, but on trying the lot he received direction to wait for the present in Savannah.

While Böhler was making his attempt among the negroes, some changes were taking place in the Savannah Congregation. He had been very much distressed by the condition he found when he arrived, for owing partly to their many difficulties and partly to Seifert's absence among the Indians, no Communion had been celebrated for a year, and the "bands" had been dropped. The Bible and prayer gatherings were steadily observed, but it seemed to him there was a lack of harmony among the members, and they were by no means ready to take him at once into their confidence. Seifert, too, was not well, and had been obliged to leave the Indians, and return to Savannah.

The Indian work was most discouraging, for the men were careless and drunken, and in January,

1739, even Rose gave up, and moved back to Savannah with his family. In October, Tomochichi died, and was buried with great pomp in Percival Square in Savannah. The Moravians were asked to furnish music at the funeral, but declined, and it was hardly missed amid the firing of minute guns, and three volleys over his grave. After his death his little village was abandoned, and the question of further missionary efforts there settled itself.

During the winter John Regnier became deeply incensed at some plain speaking from Schulius, and decided to leave at once for Europe, the Congregation paying his way. He probably went to Herrnhut, as that had been his intention some months previously, and later he served as a missionary in Surinam. In after years he returned to Pennsylvania, where he joined those who were inimical to the Moravians.

Peter Rose, his wife and daughter left for Pennsylvania soon after their withdrawal from Irene. They settled in Germantown, and there Peter died March 12th, 1740. Catherine married John Michael Huber in 1742, who died five years later on a voyage to the West Indies. Being for the third time a widow, she became one of the first occupants of the Widows' House in Bethlehem, and served as a Deaconess for many years, dying in 1798. Mary Magdalena became the wife of Rev. Paul Peter Bader in 1763.

On August 10th, 1739, John Michael Schober died after a brief illness, the ninth of the Moravian colonists to find their final resting place beside the Savannah River.

In September, General Oglethorpe received instructions to make reprisals on the Spanish for their depredations on the southern borders of the Georgia Province. He rightly judged this to be the precursor of open hostilities, and hastened his preparations to put Carolina and Georgia in a state of defense. In October the British Government declared war on Spain, and November witnessed the beginning of fighting in the Colonies. Of course this meant a re-opening of the old discussion as to the Moravians' liability for service, a repetition of the old arguments, and a renewal of the popular indignation. Oglethorpe was fairly considerate of them, thought Zinzendorf ought to have provided for two men, but added that he did not want the Moravians driven away. Still the situation was uncomfortable, and the Moravians began to make arrangements for their final departure.

By this time Böhler had won his way into the confidence of the Savannah congregation, and had learned that he was not the only one who had the Lord's interests at heart. With Seifert again in charge of affairs, the religious services had taken on new life, and on October 18th, John Martin Mack was confirmed. Judith Töltschig, however, gave them great concern, and her brother Michael Haberland sided with her, so that the company gladly saw them sail for Germany in the latter part of January, 1740. There Michael married, and returned to America in May, 1749, as one of the large company which came to settle in Bethlehem, where he died in 1783. Judith joined her husband in England, and in 1742 was serving as "sick-waiter" of the Pilgrim Congregation in London.

This left only six Moravians in Savannah, for John Böhner had already started for Pennsylvania on January 20th. He had a very sore arm which they hoped would be benefited by the change, and he was commissioned to try and gather together the members who had preceded him, and to make arrangements for the reception of the remnant which was soon to follow. He aided faithfully during the early days of the settlement at Nazareth and Bethlehem, and in 1742 went as a missionary to the island of St. Thomas, where he labored earnestly and successfully for the rest of his life, and died in 1787.

Nothing now remained for the members still in Savannah, but to so arrange matters that they might leave on the first opportunity. Oglethorpe had already bought their trumpets and French horns at a good price, but they needed to sell their rice and household furniture to provide sufficient funds for their journey. This was happily arranged on the 2d of February, when George Whitefield, who had reached Savannah for the second time a few days before, came to see them, promised to buy all they cared to sell, and offered them free passage to Pennsylvania. This offer they gratefully accepted, receiving £37 for their household goods, and on April 13th, 1740, they sailed with Whitefield on his sloop the *Savannah,* Captain Thomas Gladman. Their land and improvements were left in the hands of an Agent, and the town house was rented to some of Whitefield's followers for a hospital.

With the Moravians went the two boys, Benjamin Somers and James ...., who had been given into their hands by the Savannah magistrates in 1735, and a young woman, Johanna Hummel, of Purisburg. The two lads gave them much trouble in Pennsylvania, and Benjamin was finally bound out in 1748, while James ran away. Johanna married John Böhner, and sailed with him to the West Indies in 1742, but died at sea before reaching there.

Böhler and his company expected to find Spangenberg and Bishop Nitschmann in Pennsylvania, and were much disappointed to learn that both were absent. They scarcely knew what to do, but Böhler held them together, and when Whitefield decided to buy a large tract of land and build thereon a Negro school, and a town for his English friends of philanthropic mind, and when the Moravians were offered the task of erecting the first house there, Böhler and his companions gladly accepted the work. Bethlehem followed in due time, and all were among those who organized that congregation. David Zeisberger, Sr., died there in 1744, his wife in 1746. Anton Seifert was appointed Elder, or Pastor of the Bethlehem Congregation, married, and took an active part in the Church and School work there and at Nazareth, the latter tract having been purchased from Whitefield in 1741. April 8th, 1745, he sailed for Europe, laboring in England, Ireland and Holland, and dying at Zeist in 1785.

John Martin Mack became one of the leaders of the Moravian Church in its Mission work among the Indians in New York, Connecticut and Ohio until 1760, when he was sent to the negro slaves on St.

Thomas, preaching also on St. Croix and St. Jan, and the English West Indies. He was ordained to the ministry November 13th, 1742, and was consecrated bishop October 18th, 1770, during a visit to Pennsylvania, this being the first Episcopal consecration in the American Province of the Moravian Church. He was married four times, his last wife passing away two years before his departure. He died June 9th, 1784, and was buried in the presence of a great concourse of people,—negro converts, planters, government officers and the Governor-General.

David Zeisberger, Jr, lived a life so abundant in labors, so picturesque in experiences that a brief outline utterly fails to give any conception of it. "The apostle of the Western Indians traversed Massachusetts and Connecticut, New York, Pennsylvania and Ohio, entered Michigan and Canada, preaching to many nations in many tongues. He brought the Gospel to the Mohicans and Wampanoags, to the Nanticokes and Shawanese, to the Chippewas, Ottowas and Wyandots, to the Unamis, Unalachtgos and Monseys of the Delaware race, to the Onondagas, Cayugas and Senecas of the Six Nations. Speaking the Delaware language fluently, as well as the Mohawk and Onondaga dialects of the Iroquois; familiar with the Cayuga and other tongues; an adopted sachem of the Six Nations; naturalized among the Monseys by a formal act of the tribe; swaying for a number of years the Grand Council of the Delawares; at one time Keeper of the Archives of the Iroquois Confederacy; versed in the cus-

ZEISBERGER PREACHING TO THE INDIANS.

toms of the aborigines; adapting himself to their mode of thought, and, by long habit, a native in many of his ways;—no Protestant missionary and few men of any other calling, ever exercised more real influence and was more sincerely honored among the Indians; and no one, except the Catholic evangelists, with whom the form of baptism was the end of their work, exceeded him in the frequency and hardships of his journeys through the wilderness, the numbers whom he received into the Church of Christ, and brought to a consistent practice of Christianity, and conversion of characters most depraved, ferocious and desperate." "Nor must we look upon Zeisberger as a missionary only; he was one of the most notable pioneers of civilization our country has ever known. * * * Thirteen villages sprang up at his bidding, where native agents prepared the way for the husbandman and the mechanic of the coming race." "He was not only bold in God, fearless and full of courage, but also lowly of heart, meek of spirit, never thinking highly of himself. Selfishness was unknown to him. His heart poured out a stream of love to his fellowmen. In a word, his character was upright, honest, loving and noble, as free from faults as can be expected of any man this side of the grave."*

He died at Goshen, Ohio, Nov. 17th, 1808, having labored among the Indians for sixty years.

Like Spangenberg, Peter Böhler's story belongs to the whole Moravian Church, rather than to the Georgia colony. His time was divided between

---

*"Life and Times of David Zeisberger," by Rt. Rev. Edmund de Schweinitz.

England and America in both of which spheres he labored most successfully. Jan. 10th, 1748, he was consecrated bishop at Marienborn, Germany. After Zinzendorf's death he helped frame the new Church constitution, and in 1769 was elected to the governing board of the entire Unitas Fratrum. He died in London, April 20th, 1774, having been there for a year on a visitation to the English congregations of the Moravian Church.

Chapter VII.

CONCLUSION.

LATER ATTEMPTS IN GEORGIA.

1740.

May 18th, 1740, John Hagen arrived in Savannah. He had come over intending to go as missionary to the Cherokees, and his disappointment in finding that the Moravians had abandoned Georgia is another example of the enormous difficulty under which mission work was conducted in those days, when the most momentous events might transpire months before the authorities at home could be apprised of them.

Hagen had become very ill on the way from Charleston to Savannah, and with none of his own people to turn to he bethought himself of Whitefield's offers of friendship, and went to his house. He was kindly received by those who were living there, and though he went down to the gates of death the portals did not open, and he rapidly regained his health.

Visiting Irene he found only a few Indian women, for Tomochichi was dead, and the men were all on the warpath. The opportunity of going to the Cherokees seemed very doubtful, for there were none living nearer than three hundred miles, and distances looked much greater in the Georgia forests than in his own populous Germany. So he concluded to accept the kind offers of Whitefield's household, and stay with them, making himself useful in the garden, and doing such religious work as he was able. Several Germans living in the town, who had learned to like the Moravians, asked him to hold services for them, to which he gladly agreed.

He was much pleased with the prospect for work in Savannah, where the people had been greatly stirred by Whitefield's preaching, and he wrote to Herrnhut urging that two married couples be sent to help reap the harvest, a request warmly seconded by Whitefield, who had returned to Savannah on June 16th. Whitefield reported the Moravians busily engaged in erecting a Negro school-house for him in Pennsylvania, and told Hagen he would like to have the two couples come to assist him in carrying out his large plans for Georgia.

But by the 14th of August this invitation had been withdrawn, Hagen had left Whitefield's house, and had been refused work on Whitefield's plantation, for fear that he might contaminate the Whitefield converts. The trouble arose over a discussion on Predestination,—not the first or last time this has happened,—and the two men found themselves utterly at variance, for Whitefield held the extreme Calvinistic view, while Hagen argued that all men who would might be saved. Hagen therefore went to the home of John Brownfield, who shared his views, and made him very welcome, and from there carried on his work among the residents of Savannah and Purisburg.

Whitefield returned to Pennsylvania in November, 1740, nursing his wrath against Hagen, and finding Böhler to be of the same mind, he peremptorily ordered the Moravians to leave his land. Neighbors interfered, and cried shame on him for turning the little company adrift in the depth of winter, and he finally agreed to let them stay for awhile in the log cabin which was sheltering them while they were building the large stone house. The opportune arrival of Bishop Nitschmann and his company, and the purchase of the Bethlehem tract, soon relieved them from their uncomfortable position, and later the Nazareth tract was bought from Whitefield, and the work they had begun for him was completed for their own use.

Whitefield, in after years, rather excused himself for his first harshness toward the Moravians, but a letter written by him to a friend in 1742, is a good statement of the armed truce which existed among the great religious leaders of that day. "Where the spirit of God is in any great degree, there will be union of avail, tho' there may be difference in sentiments. This I have learnt, my dear Brother, by happy experience, and find great freedom and peace in my soul thereby. This makes me love the Moravian Brethren tho' I cannot agree with them in many of their principles. I cannot look upon them as willful deceivers, but as persons who hazard their lives for the sake of the Gospel. Mr. Wesley is as certainly wrong in some things as they, and Mr. Law as wrong also. Yet I believe both Mr. Law and Mr. Wesley and the Count Zinzendorf will shine bright in Glory. I have not given way to the Moravian Brethren, nor any other who I thought were in the wrong, no, not for one hour. But I think it best not to dispute when there is no probability of convincing."

Hagen remained in Savannah until February, 1742, when he went to Bethlehem, accompanied by Abraham Büninger, of Purisburg, who entered the Moravian ministry in 1742, and labored among the Indians, the white settlers, and in the West Indies.

Nine more residents of Georgia followed the Moravians to Bethlehem in 1745, John Brownfield, James Burnside and his daughter Rebecca, Henry Ferdinand Beck, his wife Barbara, their daughter Maria Christina, and their sons Jonathan and David, all of Savannah, and Anna Catharine Kremper, of Purisburg. All of these served faithfully in various important offices, and were valuable fruit of the efforts in Georgia.

John Hagen was appointed Warden of the Nazareth congregation, when it was organized; and died at Shamokin in 1747.

1746.

General Oglethorpe was much impressed by the industry of the Moravians in Savannah, and was sorry to see them leave the Province. In October, 1746, therefore, he proposed to Count Zinzendorf that a new attempt should be made further up the Savannah River. He offered to give them five hundred and twenty-six acres near Purisburg, and to arrange for two men to be stationed in Augusta, either as licensed Traders, for many Indians came there, or as Schoolmasters.

Zinzendorf thought well of the plan, and accepted

the tract, which Oglethorpe deeded to him Nov. 1st, 1746, the land lying on the Carolina side of the Savannah River, adjoining the township of Purisburg, where Böhler and Schulius had made many friends.

No colonists, however, were sent over, and the title to the land lapsed for lack of occupancy, as that to Old Fort, on the Ogeechee, had already done.

1774.

Early in 1774 Mr. Knox, Under-Secretary of State in London, asked for missionaries to preach the Gospel to the slaves on his plantation in Georgia. He offered a small piece of land, whereon they might live independently, and promised ample store of provisions.

This time the plan was carried into execution, and Ludwig Müller, formerly teacher in the Pedagogium at Niesky, with John George Wagner as his companion, went to England, and sailed from there to Georgia. They settled on Mr. Knox's plantation, and at once began to visit and instruct the slaves, and preach to the whites living in the neighborhood. "Knoxborough" lay on a creek about sixteen miles from Savannah, midway between that town and Ebenezer. The land had been settled by Germans, Salzburgers and Wittenbergers, and Mr. Knox had bought up their fifty acre tracts, combining them into a large rice plantation. The homes of the Germans had been allowed to fall into ruin, the overseer occupying a three-roomed house, with an outside kitchen. Müller was given a room in the overseer's house, preaching there to the white neighbors who chose to hear him, and to the negroes in the large shed that sheltered the stamping mill. Wagner occupied a room cut off from the kitchen.

In February, 1775, Frederick William Marshall, Agent of the Unitas Fratrum on the Wachovia Tract in North Carolina, (with headquarters at Salem) visited Georgia to inspect the Moravian property there, accompanied by Andrew Brösing, who joined Müller and Wagner in their missionary work. It had been suggested that the Moravians preach in a church at a little place called Goshen, near "Knoxborough," a church which had been built by subscriptions of Germans and English living in the neighborhood, and had been used occasionally by a preacher from Ebenezer.

At this time the Salzburgers were in a very bad condition. Bolzius had died in 1765, and Rabenhorst and Triebner, who shared the pastorate, were greatly at variance, so that the entire settlement was split into factions. Dr. Mühlenberg, "the father of Lutheranism in Pennsylvania," had come to settle the difficulties, and heard with much displeasure of the plan to have the Moravians preach at Goshen. He declared,—"I doubt not, according to their known method of insinuation, they will gain the most, if not all the remaining families in Goshen, and will also make an attempt on Ebenezer, for their ways are well adapted to awakened souls. I have learned by experience that where strife and disunion have occurred in neighborhoods and congregations among the Germans in America, there black and white apostles have immediately appeared, and tried to fish in the troubled waters, like eagles which have a keen sight and smell."

Dr. Mühlenberg was too much prejudiced against the Moravians to judge them fairly, for he belonged to the Halle party in Germany, and in Pennsylvania had clashed with Zinzendorf during the latter's residence there. The Lutheran Church was in no way endangered by the preaching of the missionaries, for their instructions were explicit: "If you have an opportunity to preach the Gospel to German or English residents use it gladly, but receive none into your congregation, for you are sent expressly to the negroes." "You will probably find some of the so-called Salzburgers there, with their ministers. With them you will in all fairness do only that to which you are invited by their pastor. You will do nothing in their congregation that you would not like to have another do in yours." Dr. Mühlenberg, therefore, might safely have left them free to preach the Gospel where they would, even to his own distracted flock, which was weakened by dissensions, suffered severely in the Revolutionary War, and gradually scattered into the adjoining country.

In accordance with his instructions, Müller at once gave up all idea of using the Goshen church, and occupied himself with those who heard him gladly at Knoxborough. After a careful examination of the land, the Moravians decided not to build a house for themselves, but to continue with the overseer, who was kind to them, and gave Müller the use of a horse for his visits to adjoining plantations.

James Habersham, who had come over with George Whitefield in 1738, was one of the most prominent men in Savannah at this time. In 1744 he had established a commercial house in Georgia, the first of its kind, to ship lumber, hogs, skins, etc., to England, and this business had been a success. He had taken a great interest in Whitefield's Orphan House, and had been active in governmental affairs, having served as Secretary of the Province, President of the Council, and Acting Governor of Georgia. For many years he had been the Agent in charge of the Moravian lots in and near Savannah, and now, in failing health, and a sufferer from gout, he asked that one of the missionaries might be sent to his three estates on the Ogeechee River, partly as his representative and partly to instruct the slaves. It was decided that Wagner should accept this invitation and go to "Silkhope," while Müller and Brösing remained at Knoxborough, Müller preaching at "Silkhope" every two weeks.

Marshall was much pleased with the reception accorded him and the missionaries, and hoped the time was coming for again using the lots in Savannah, but the hope again proved to be fallacious. The missionaries all suffered greatly from fever, always prevalent on the rice plantations in the summer, and on Oct. 11th, 1775, Müller died. The outbreak of the Revolutionary War made Wagner's and Brösing's position precarious, for the English Act exempting the Moravians from military service was not likely to be respected by the Americans, and in 1776 Brösing returned to Wachovia, where the Moravians had settled in sufficient numbers to hold their own, though amid trials manifold. Wagner stayed in Georgia until 1779, and then he too left the field, and returned to England.

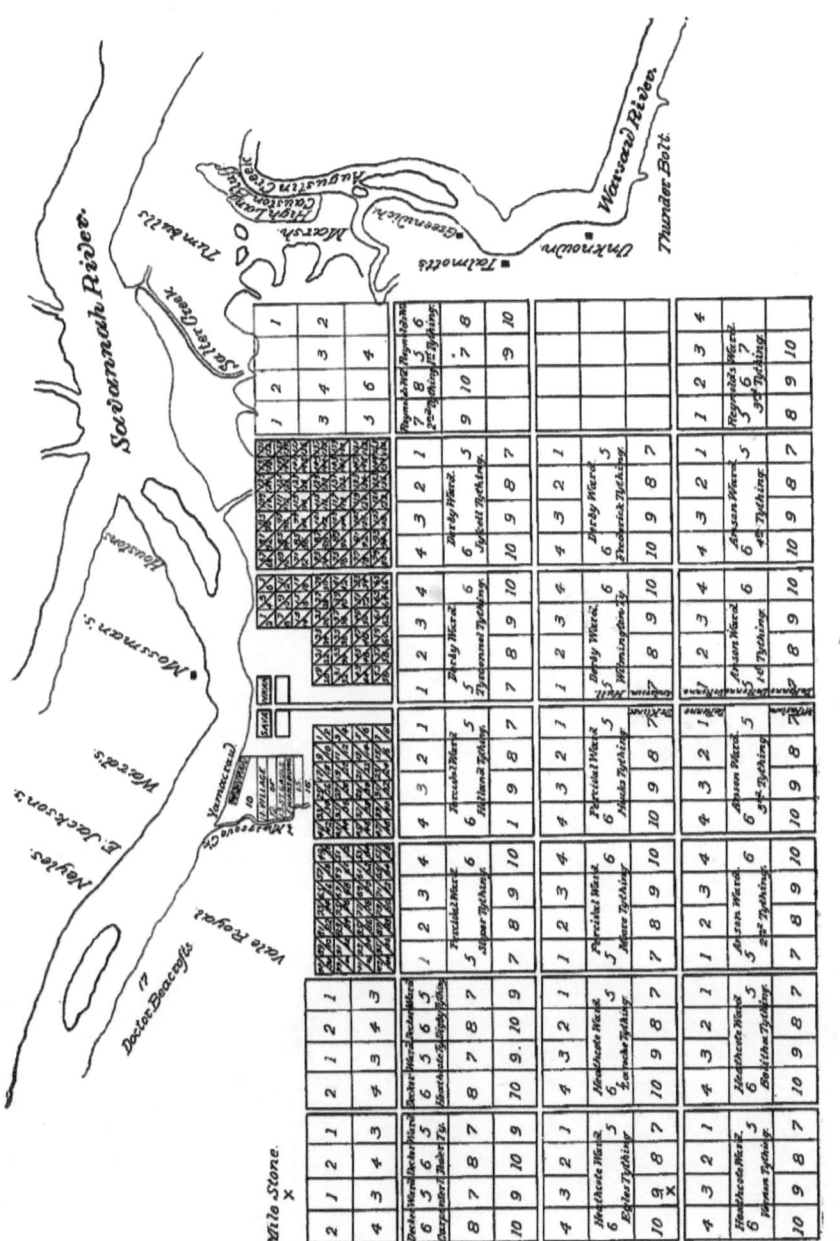

SAVANNAH AND ENVIRONS.
Town, Gardens, and Farms.

CONCLUSION. 229

THE SAVANNAH LANDS.

In January, 1735, fifty acres of Savannah land was granted by the Trustees of Georgia to August Gottlieb Spangenberg, who was going to Georgia as the leader of the first company of Moravian colonists. Spangenberg had the habit of speaking of himself as "Brother Joseph" in his diaries, and in the records he sometimes appears as Joseph Spangenberg, sometimes as Joseph Augustus Gottlieb Spangenberg, and sometimes by his true name only. According to custom, the fifty acre grant embraced three lots,—Town Lot No. 4, Second Tything, Anson Ward, in the town of Savannah, Farm Lot No. 2, Second Tything, Anson Ward, in the township of Savannah, and Garden Lot No. 120, East. (Office of the Secretary of State of Georgia, Book D of Grants, Folio 208.)

A few days later a similar grant was made to David Nitschmann, "Count Zinzendorf's Hausmeister," generally known as the Syndic from his office in later years, who had conducted the first company from Herrnhut to London. This grant consisted of Town Lot No. 3, Second Tything, Anson Ward, in the town of Savannah, Farm Lot No. 3, Second Tything, Anson Ward, in the township of Savannah, and Garden Lot No. 121 East. (Office of Secretary of State of Georgia, Book D of Grants, Folio 207.)

When the Moravians left Georgia in 1740, these lots were placed in the hands of an Agent, probably James Habersham, who was acting as Whitefield's assistant in his hospital and charity school, the Moravian house being rented for the former purpose.

When the Trustees of Georgia surrendered their Charter to the English Crown in 1754, it was found that no formal deeds had ever been made for many of the tracts granted by the Trustees, and it was decreed that any who could legally claim land under grant from the Trustees should have their rights confirmed by royal grant upon application to the Governor and Council of Georgia, within a specified time, the land otherwise to be considered forfeited. In June, 1761, Habersham wrote to Bethlehem that the time for entering claim had expired, but that he had asked for and obtained six months grace for the Moravians, who had previously sent him a full power of attorney, which had failed to reach him.

A new power of attorney was at once sent, and on September 7th, 1762, royal patents were issued to Nitschmann and Spangenberg, for the Town Lots and Farm Lots above mentioned. (Register's Office, Book D, Folios 207 and 208.)

Meanwhile the two Garden Lots had been sold to Sir James Wright for £10, and deeds, bearing date of March 15th, 1762, were made to him by Spangenberg and Nitschmann. The deeds to the Town and Farm lots were deposited in Bethlehem, and the Agent took his instructions from the Manager there.

In 1765 Bishop Ettwein went from Bethlehem to Savannah to look after the property. He found that the large house on Spangenberg's lot had been condemned as ruinous and pulled down. Some one had built a small house on the other end of the same lot, and it was supposed to pay £4 a year ground rent, but the family living there was very poor, and Habersham had been unable to collect anything. By

JAMES HABERSHAM.

permission a poor woman had fenced in the Nitschmann lot, and was using it as a kitchen-garden, rent free. The title to the farm lots was in jeopardy, for a certain Alderman Becker in London claimed that the Trustees had given him a tract, including these and many other farms, but the settlers thereon were making a strong fight to hold their property, in which they were finally successful.

At the time of Frederick William Marshall's visit to Savannah in 1775, the two farm lots were reported to have some good timber, even if they were not of much use otherwise, and the town lots had increased in value with the growth of the town. Marshall thought the latter could again be used for residence, and as a centre for such missionary work as was already begun by Müller, Wagner and Brösing, but the Revolutionary War put an end to their efforts.

At this point in the records appears a peculiar uncertainty as to the identity of the owner of the David Nitschmann lots. The fact that there were three David Nitschmanns in the active service of the Moravian Church during a number of years after its renewal in Herrnhut affords ample opportunity for confusion, but one would not expect to find it in the minds of their contemporaries. But even such a man as Frederick William Marshall wrote, "The Deeds to these two lots, Nos. 3 and 4, are kept in Bethlehem (one stands in the name of Brother Joseph, the other of Bishop D'd Nitschmann, who passed away in Bethlehem) and it would be well if something were done about them. I do not know what can be arranged with the son of the latter; but Brother David Nitschmann, who is now in Zeist, said when he was in America that he himself was the David Nitschmann in whose name the grant was made, because he was the one who had shared in the negotiations with the Trustees of Georgia." Bishop David Nitschmann had died in Bethlehem, Oct. 9th, 1772, where his son Immanuel lived until 1790. The David Nitschmann residing in Zeist was the Syndic, formerly Count Zinzendorf's Hausmeister, the leader of the first company to London, where he and Spangenberg had arranged matters with the Trustees, and had each received fifty acres of land in his own name. The Bishop had had nothing whatever to do with the matter, and this was the conclusion reached, for the title to the Town Lot No. 3 passed at the Syndic's death, March 28th, 1779, to his son Christian David Nitschmann.

June 14th, 1784, August Gottlieb Spangenberg and Christian David Nitschmann by deed transferred their title to the Savannah property to Hans Christian Alexander von Schweinitz, Administrator of the estate of the Unitas Fratrum in Pennsylvania.

The Revolutionary War had come and gone, and Von Schweinitz began again to investigate the condition of affairs in Savannah. Their Agent, James Habersham, had died in 1775, but his son James had kept up the taxes, so the title was intact. "But there is a matter," he wrote, "which it is necessary you should be made acquainted with. When the British Troops took possession of Savannah, they had occasion for a lot belonging to a Mr. George Kellar, for the purpose of erecting a fort on, it being situated in the outskirts of the town, and in order to satisfy this man they *very generously* gave him your two lots in lieu of the one they had taken from him, but very fortunately for you, our Legislature passed a Law rendering null and void all their acts during the time they held this country, and notwithstanding Mr. Kellar is perfectly well acquainted with this matter, he has moved a house on one of the lots, and on the other he has lately built another house, which he rents out, and holds possession—in defiance of me, as I am possessed of no power of attorney to warrant any proceeding against him." A power of attorney was at once sent Habersham, with instructions to evict the intruder, and rent, lease or sell the property.

A suit against the trespasser was won in 1794, but in 1801 his tenant was still in possession, poor, and refusing to pay rent. Habersham had meanwhile died, and John Gebhard Cunow, acting as attorney for Von Schweinitz, who had returned to Germany in 1798, requested Matthew McAllister to take charge of the matter; but McAllister, having made some inquiries, reported that the man named John Robinson, who lived on the premises, was likely to make trouble, and that as he himself was the only Judge in the district it would be better to put the case into the hands of some one else, and leave him free to hear it. Cunow therefore asked George Woodruff to act as attorney, to which he agreed, requesting that John Lawson be associated with him, which was done the following year.

Hans Christian Alexander von Schweinitz died Feb. 26th, 1802, the title to the Savannah Lots passing by will to Christian Lewis Benzien, of Salem, North Carolina, who however requested Cunow to continue to look after them.

The Agents had no light task in ejecting John Robinson and his wife from their abode, for he was "a foolish, drunken man," and she "a perfect *virago*, and the Sheriff is really afraid of her," but on July 5th, 1805, Lawson wrote to Cunow,—"I am happy to inform you that after great trouble and difficulty we have this day obtained possession of Mr. Benzien's lots."

Feb. 17th, 1807, Christian Lewis Benzien, by his attorneys Woodruff and Lawson, conveyed Town Lot No. 4, Second Tything, Anson Ward, to Charles Odingsell, the consideration being $1,500, one hundred dollars in cash, the rest secured by bond and mortgage, payable in one, two, and three years, with 8 per cent interest from date.

In the same manner Town Lot No. 3 was sold to Worthington Gale, March 14th, 1807, for $1,450.

Owing to "the distress of the times," payment of these bonds was slightly delayed, but by June, 1811, both were cancelled.

Although the two Town Lots thus brought $2,950, they had cost a good deal in taxes and attorney's fees, and it is doubtful whether the general treasury profited greatly by the investment, and certainly the men who had lived and labored and suffered in Georgia were in no financial way enriched thereby.

Christian Lewis Benzien died Nov. 13th, 1811, and the two Farm Lots were transferred by will to John Gebhard Cunow of Bethlehem, Pa., who in

March, 1822, deeded them to Lewis David de Schweinitz of Bethlehem, Pa.

And here the two Farm Lots disappear from the records. They had never been available for farming purposes, and by degrees the timber was stolen from them, so that it became wiser to let them go than to keep up the taxes with no prospect of return. In course of time the title lapsed, and the land passed uncontested into other hands.

ARRIVALS IN GEORGIA.

April	6th, 1735.	August Gottlieb Spangenberg	From Germany.
"	"	John Töltschig	"
"	7th,	Peter Rose	"
"	"	Gotthard Demuth	"
"	"	Gottfried Haberecht	"
"	"	Anton Seifert	"
"	"	Michael Haberland	"
"	"	George Haberland	"
"	"	George Waschke	"
"	"	Friedrich Riedel	"
Oct.	11th,	John Regnier	From Pennsylvania.
Feb.	17th, 1736.	David Nitschmann, (the Bishop)	From Germany.
"	23rd	Christian Adolph von Hermsdorf	"
"	"	Henry Roscher	"
"	"	John Andrew Dober	"
"	"	Maria Catharine Dober, (wife of Andrew D.)	"
"	"	George Neisser	"
"	"	Augustin Neisser	"
"	"	David Zeisberger	"
"	"	Rosina Zeisberger, (wife of David Z.)	"
"	"	David Tanneberger	"

ARRIVALS IN GEORGIA.

Feb. 23rd, 1736.	John Tanneberger, (son of David T.)	From Germany.
" "	David Jag	"
" "	John Michael Meyer	"
" "	Jacob Frank	"
" "	John Martin Mack	"
" "	Matthias Seybold	"
" "	Gottlieb Demuth	"
" "	John Böhner	"
" "	Matthias Böhnisch	"
" "	Regina Demuth, (wife of Gotthard D.)	"
" "	Judith Töltschig, (wife of John T.)	"
" "	Catharine Riedel, (wife of Friedrich R.)	"
" "	Anna Waschke, (mother of George W.)	"
" "	Juliana Jäschke	"
" "	Rosina Haberecht, (wife of Gottfried H.)	"
Sept. 16th, 1737.	Anna Catherina Rose, } (daughters of Peter R.)	"
" "	Maria Magdalena Rose, }	
Jan. 28th, 1738.	David Zeisberger, Jr.	From Holland.
" "	John Michael Schober	"
Oct. 16th, "	Peter Böhler, (missionary to negroes)	From Germany.
" "	George Schulius, (assistant missionary)	"

ARRIVALS IN GEORGIA—Continued.

Oct. 16th, 1738.	Simon Peter Harper	From England.
May 18th, 1740.	John Hagen	From Germany.
Autumn, 1774.	Ludwig Müller	"
"	John George Wagner	"
March 5th, 1775.	Andrew Brösing	From North Carolina.

DEPARTURES FROM GEORGIA.

March 15th, 1736.	August Gottlieb Spangenberg	To Pennsylvania.
March 26th, 1736.	Bishop David Nitschmann	"
Dec. 2nd, 1736.	John Andrew Dober	To Germany.
"	Maria Catherine Dober	"
March 9th, 1737.	George Neisser	To Pennsylvania.
May 16th, 1737.	Christian Adolph von Hermsdorf	To Germany.
Oct. 16th, 1737.	David Tanneberger	To Pennsylvania.
"	John Tanneberger	"
"	John Michael Meyer	"
"	Gottfried Haberecht	"
End of Jan., 1738.	Gotthard Demuth	"
"	Regina Demuth	"
"	George Waschke	"

Departures from Georgia.

End of Jan., 1738.	Juliana Waschke	To Pennsylvania.
"	Anna Waschke	"
"	Augustin Neisser	"
"	Gottlieb Demuth	"
"	David Jag	"
March 12th, 1738.	John Töltschig	To Europe.
Summer, "	Matthias Seybold	To Pennsylvania.
Winter, 1738–39.	John Francis Regnier	To Germany.
" 1739.	Peter Rose	To Pennsylvania.
" "	Catherine Rose	"
" "	Maria Magdalena Rose	"
" "	Simon Peter Harper	"
Jan. 20th, 1740.	John Böhner	To Pennsylvania.
Jan., 1740.	Judith Töltschig	To Germany.
" "	Michael Haberland	"
April 13th, 1740.	Peter Böhler	To Pennsylvania.
" "	Anton Seifert	"
" "	John Martin Mack	"
" "	David Zeisberger	"
" "	Rosina Zeisberger	"
" "	David Zeisberger, Jr.	"

DEPARTURES FROM GEORGIA—Continued.

Feb.,	1742.	John Hagen	....	To Pennsylvania.
April 13th,	1740.	Benjamin Somers	....	"
"	"	James	....	"
"	"	Johanna Hummel	....	"
Feb.,	1742.	Abraham Büninger	....	"
	1744.	James Burnside	....	"
	"	Rebecca Burnside	....	"
	1745.	John Brownfield	....	"
	"	Henry Ferdinand Beck	....	"
	"	Barbara Beck	....	"
	"	Maria Christina Beck	....	"
	"	Jonathan Beck	....	"
	"	David Beck	....	"
	"	Anna Catherina Kremper	....	"
	1776.	Andrew Brösing	....	To North Carolina.
May,	1779.	John George Wagner	....	To England.

DEATHS.

Oct. 11th, 1735.	Friedrich Riedel	In Savannah.
March 19th, 1736.	Jacob Frank	"
March 30th, 1736.	Henry Roscher	"
June 17th, "	Rosina Haberecht	"
Oct. 3rd, "	Matthias Böhnisch	"
Sept. 30th, 1737.	George Haberland	"
(Nov.?) "	Anna Catherina Rose	"
Aug. 4th, 1739.	George Schulius	In Purisburg.
Aug. 10th, "	John Michael Schober	In Savannah.
Oct. 11th, 1775.	Ludwig Müller	At Knoxborough.

SUMMARY.

Arrivals.

From Europe	43
" Pennsylvania	1
Born in Georgia	2
From North Carolina	1
	—— 47

Deaths.

At Savannah	8
At Purisburg	1
At Knoxborough	1
	—— 10

Departures.

To Bethlehem, Pa.	18
To other Moravian Congregations in America	3
To Moravian Congregations in Europe	8
Scattered	8
	—— 37
	—— 47

Following the Moravians from Georgia to Bethlehem... 13

INDEX.

A.

	PAGE.
Act of Parliament	187, 199, 228
Aeltester	133, 138, 154, 175, 185
Allen, Brierly	186
Altamaha River	121, 123, 127, 128, 129, 130, 162
Anna	156
Anthony	37
Altona	42, 91, 92
Arrivals in Georgia	236, 237, 238, 242
Associates of the late Dr. Bray	202, 203, 204, 211, 213
Augsburg	19, 20
Augusta	224

B.

Bader, Paul Peter	214
Bands	103, 129, 177, 196, 200, 213
Beck, Barbara	224
Beck, David	224
Beck, Henry Ferdinand	224
Beck, Jonathan	224
Beck, Maria Christina	224
Benzien, Christian Lewis	234
Berthelsdorf	26, 140
Bethlehem	136, 184, 188, 201, 214–217, 223, 224, 230, 231, 235
Bohemia	21, 23, 29, 41, 45, 46, 48, 92
Böhler, Peter	189–192, 194, 199, 202–213, 215, 217, 219, 220, 223, 226
Böhner, John	92, 107, 150, 156, 185, 208, 216, 217
Böhnisch, George	34, 141
Böhnisch, Matthias	92, 157
Bolzius, Martin	20, 44, 46, 82, 178, 226
Bray, Thomas	203
Brösing, Andrew	226, 228, 231
Brother Joseph	42, 229, 231
Brownfield, John	222, 224
Büninger, Abraham	224
Burnside, James	224
Burnside, Rebecca	224

C.

Calendar	100
Calvin, John	21
Carolina	14, 72, 79, 141, 161, 162, 163, 183, 203, 210, 213
Causton, Thomas	66, 68, 84, 163, 164, 167, 168, 182, 185

	PAGE.
Charles II	13
Charles V	19
Charleston 20, 140, 141, 147, 163, 186, 189, 210, 213	
Cherokees	149, 221
Chief Elder	See Aeltester.
Christ Church	143
Church of England 53, 99, 132, 140, 144, 145, 191, 197, 206	
Collegiants	35, 36
Comenius, John Amos	21
Comfort	156
Committee for relief of Debtors	13, 14
Confession of Faith, Moravian	27
Coram, Thomas	35, 47
Cornish, Capt.	97, 101, 114
Creek Confederacy	148
Cunow, John Gebhard	233, 234

D.

Deaths	241, 242
Delamotte, Charles 99, 101, 104, 105, 109, 131, 144, 168, 186, 202	
Demuth, Gotthard	48, 69, 79, 83, 129, 188
Demuth, Gottlieb	92, 156, 188
Demuth, Regina	92, 112, 184, 188
Departures from Georgia	238, 239, 240, 242
Diener	129, 139, 174, 175, 185
Dober, John Andrew....... 92, 99, 101, 103, 106, 108, 129, 131, 155, 159, 181	
Dober, Leonard	90
Dober, Maria Catherine	92, 103, 156, 159
Dunbar, Capt.	140
Düsseldorf	26

E.

Ebenezer, New	127, 178, 202, 225, 226
Ebenezer, Old	20, 44, 75, 88, 125
Ebersdorf	50
Ecce Homo	26
Ecclesiolae in ecclesia	24
Eckstein, John	170, 181
Egede, Hans	37
Elders	138
England.............. See Moravian Activity in England.	
English School at Herrnhut	95
Ephrata	184
Episcopate of Unitas Fratrum.... 22, 90, 91, 107, 133, 134, 140, 145, 160, 218	

INDEX. 245

	PAGE.
Ermahner	129
Ettwein, John	230
Exile Hymn	49

F.

Farm Lots 16, 52, 77, 78, 79, 180, 229–232, 234, 235
Fetter Lane Congregation........................ 199, 200
Fetter Lane Society 191, 194, 195, 196, 199, 205
Fifty Acre Tracts..................... 51, 52, 78, 126, 229
Financial affairs 30–34, 38, 43, 44, 45, 50, 51, 53,
                71, 72, 78, 84, 89, 95, 96, 107, 109, 129, 135,
                136, 137, 155, 165, 168, 173, 180, 181, 182,
                184, 189, 190, 216, 230, 234.
First Company 47–56, 67, 70, 139, 229
Five Acre Lots.........................see Garden Lots.
Five Hundred Acre Tract.....................see Old Fort.
Five Hundred Acre Tract (2nd)..................... 94, 126
Five Hundred and Twenty-six Acre Tract............. 224
Florida 162
Foreign Missions 37, 38, 43, 160, 221
Fort Argyle .... 72—76
Forty-five Acre Lots........................see Farm Lots.
Foundry Society 196
Frank, Jacob 92, 138, 179
Frederica 127, 128, 130, 143, 144, 145, 147, 158, 201
Fulneck 198

G.

Gale, Worthington 234
Gambold, John 206
Garden Lots........ 16, 52, 68, 69, 77, 78, 79, 122, 180,
                                                229, 230
Gascoine, Capt. 107
Gemeinschaft 135, 136, 155, 158, 173, 174, 177, 179
George II.. 14
Georgia..... 13–18, 20, 29, 30, 33, 35, 36, 38, 43, 44, 68,
        77, 83, 95, 96, 127, 128, 162, 163, 166, 182, 210, 215,
        227, 230.
Germantown 170, 184, 188
Gladman, Capt. Thomas 216
Goshen 226, 227
Goshenhopper 188
Greenland 37
Gronav, Israel Christian..................... 20, 82, 178

H.

Haberecht, Gottfried 48, 69, 79, 83, 129, 176, 184
Haberecht, Rosina 92, 157
Haberland, George 48, 69, 79, 158, 185

PAGE.
Haberland, Michael 48, 73, 79, 185, 208, 215
Habersham, James, Jr. 232, 233
Habersham, James, Sr. 202, 216, 227, 229, 230, 232
Hagen, John 221-224
Halle 20, 25, 39-43, 71, 193, 194, 227
Harper, Simon Peter...................... 202, 206, 211
Hawk, The 106, 107, 109, 110
Helfer ....see Helpers.
Helpers 138, 139
Herbert, Henry 143
Hermsdorf, Christian Adolph von.... 91, 94, 106, 121,
 123, 128, 133, 158, 173
Herrnhut...... 23, 25-29, 37, 39, 42, 43, 45, 58, 71, 90,
 92, 95, 105, 120, 135, 150, 165, 176, 188, 192, 193,
 194, 200, 201.
Holland................see Moravian Activity in Holland.
Hourly Intercession 58, 67
Household Affairs 69, 83-86, 131, 132, 135, 136,
 155, 156, 158, 172, 173, 174, 179, 201, 216
Huber, John Michael............................... 214
Hummel, Johanna 217
Hus, John 21, 201
Hutton, James 99, 193, 195, 198, 203

I.

Indian School House .... see Irene.
Indians in Georgia....... 15, 32, 45, 46, 67, 68, 70-75,
 86, 94, 99, 112, 124, 126, 127, 131, 137,
 141, 144, 147-155, 161, 162, 181, 185, 186,
 187, 198, 213.
Indians in Pa.. 217, 218
Ingham, Benjamin..... 99, 101, 104, 105, 109, 110, 112,
 121, 128, 134, 143-146, 149, 150, 152, 153,
 154, 164, 168, 169, 181, 190-193, 196-199.
Instructions 70
Ireland................see Moravian Activity in Ireland.
Irene 154, 155, 214, 221

J.

Jablonski 90, 91, 160
Jag, David 92, 156, 176, 177, 184, 188
James 217
Jäschke, Juliana 92, 157, 174, 176
Jena 25, 41, 193, 203, 208
Jews 82
Johnson .... 73—76
Journal, John Wesley's.................. 99, 101-121, 192

K.

	PAGE.
Kellar, George	232, 233
Knox, Mr.	225
Knoxborough	225–228
Koker, Pieter	35, 192
Korte, Jonas	90, 92, 93, 96, 98, 125
Krankenwärter	129
Kremper, Anna Catherine	224

L.

Laborers	200
Lamb's Hill	198
Lancashire	197
Land titles	95, 126, 161, 225, 229–235
Lawson, John	233, 234
Leopold, Archbishop of Salzburg	18
London	43, 47, 50, 54, 55, 93, 159
London Merchant, The	105, 109, 117, 118, 127
Lords Proprietors	14, 161
Lorenz	33, 34
Lot, The	139, 149, 150, 158, 165, 166, 167, 172, 175, 189, 210, 213
Lovefeasts	130, 139, 181, 196
Lower Creeks	18, 149, 152
Lutheran Church	19, 23, 25, 28, 140, 226, 227
Luther, Martin	19, 21, 28

M.

Mack, John Martin	92, 113, 215, 217
Marienborn	192, 193, 220
Marshall, Frederick William	226, 228, 231
Matrimonial affairs	156, 158, 174, 176
McAllister, Matthew	233
Melancthon	19
Methodists	99, 186, 191, 194, 196
Meyer, John Michael	92, 184
Military affairs	33, 87, 88, 93, 94, 126, 141, 161, 163–167, 172, 181, 182, 183, 186, 199, 215, 228
Moberley, Capt.	206, 207
Molther, Philip Henry	195
Moravia	21, 22, 29, 45, 46, 48, 90, 92, 166
Moravian Activity in England	41, 49, 56, 97, 160–163, 190, 194–200, 202, 205, 217, 220
Moravian Activity in Holland	35, 42, 93, 192, 217
Moravian Activity in Ireland	199, 200, 217
Moravian Congregation in Fetter Lane	see Fetter Lane Society.
Mühlenberg, Henry Melchior	226, 227
Müller, Ludwig	225–228, 231

	PAGE.
Musgrove, John	68
Musgrove, Mary	68, 131, 149
Music	214, 216

N.

Nazareth	216, 217, 223, 224
Negro Mission	201, 202, 204, 209–213, 225, 227, 228
Neisser, Augustin	92, 188
Neisser, George	92, 107, 150, 168, 169
Neisser, Wenzel	203, 204, 206
Neubert, Rosina	91
New Ebenezer	see Ebenezer, New.
New Inverness	127
Nitschmann, Christian David	232
Nitschmann, David (Bishop)	88, 90, 91, 93–99, 101, 103, 108, 111, 120, 122, 123, 129–134, 139, 141, 158, 159, 160, 184, 204, 217, 223, 231, 232.
Nitschmann, David (Hausmeister, Syndic)	39, 48, 49, 52, 53, 58, 61, 68, 78, 88, 89, 90, 94, 126, 183, 229–232.
Nitschmann, Immanuel	232
North Carolina	14
Nova Scotia	47

N.

Ober-Berthelsdorf	28, 29, 34
Odingsell, Charles	234
Oeconomie	136
Ogeechee River	72, 73, 74, 76, 225, 228
Oglethorpe, James	13, 14, 17, 20, 45, 47, 50, 51, 53, 54, 58, 72, 87, 88, 93, 94, 95, 97, 98, 99, 102, 104, 107–113, 118, 120–123, 125, 128, 129, 130, 135, 139, 143, 145, 147, 149, 152, 155, 159, 162–165, 167, 173, 188, 199, 204–207, 210–213, 215, 216, 224, 225.
Old Fort	39, 42, 47, 51, 70, 72, 73, 75, 76, 79, 94, 126, 160, 161, 164, 225
Order of the Mustard Seed	160
Orphan House	202, 228
Oxford	99, 205, 208

P.

Peeper Island (Cockspur)	120
Pennsylvania	35, 36, 91, 140, 141, 142, 168, 173, 183, 184, 187, 195, 200, 201, 214, 216, 218, 223, 227, 232.
Periagua	125, 127

INDEX.

	PAGE.
Pfeil, von	20, 33, 34, 38
Pietists	25
Pilgrim Congregation	200, 216
Poland	21, 22, 90
Port Royal	140
Potter, John, (Archbishop of Canterbury)	160, 203
Province of Georgia	see Georgia.
Pudsey	198
Purisburg	52, 208–213, 217, 222, 224, 226
Putten, Cornelius van	35

Q.

Quincy, Samuel 131, 143

R.

Ratio Disciplinae 22, 23
Reck, George Philipp Frederick von, 20, 39, 41, 97, 106, 107, 117, 125, 139
Reck, the younger 125
Regensberg 20, 34
Regnier, John 80, 81, 82, 126, 129, 137, 156, 189, 208, 214
Religious affairs ... 32, 33, 69, 70, 71, 101–108, 110, 112, 124, 127, 129, 130, 132–135, 138, 146, 155, 156, 161, 167, 174, 175, 179, 185, 187, 199, 213, 215, 218, 222, 223.
Reuss, Henry XXIX 50
Revolutionary War 227, 228, 231, 232, 233
Richter, Abraham Ehrenfried 190, 203, 204
Riedel, Catherine 92, 122, 158
Riedel, Friedrich 48, 55, 73, 79, 80, 120, 122, 158
Robinson, John 233, 234
Roman Catholics 15, 21, 107, 132, 207, 219
Roscher, Henry 92, 113, 156, 157
Rose, Anna Catherina 175
Rose, Catherine (Riedel) 152–155, 158, 185, 208, 214
Rose, Maria Magdalena 175, 185, 208, 214
Rose, Peter 48, 55, 69, 73, 74, 84, 86, 130, 152–155, 158, 174, 179, 185, 208, 214
Rothe, John Andrew 26, 140
Rotterdam 20, 35, 42
Rotten-possum 76

S.

Salem 226, 234
Salzburgers ..... 16, 18–21, 34, 39, 40, 41, 44, 46, 54, 72, 82, 88, 94, 97, 105, 109, 117, 125, 127, 178, 225, 226, 227.

INDEX.

	PAGE.
Savannah.... 18, 20, 52, 66, 72, 75, 80, 82, 87, 99, 120, 125, 163–167, 182, 186, 201, 206, 214, 222, 224	
Savannah Congregation, (Moravian).... 78, 122, 126, 129–136, 139, 145, 146, 150, 151, 153, 160, 161, 164–167, 172, 176, 177, 184, 186, 187, 198, 201, 208, 213, 215, 216	
Savannah Cemetery 80, 122, 185, 214	
Savannah River 17, 65, 119, 162, 224	
Savannah, The	216
Saxony 18, 22, 43, 45, 46	
Schober, John Michael 188, 189, 214	
Schoeneck	188
Schulius, George 190, 202–212, 214, 226	
Schwarz, Rosina	91
Schweinitz, Hans Christian Alexander von........ 232, 233	
Schweinitz, Lewis David de...............	235
Schwenkfeld, Casper	28
Schwenkfelders ... 28, 29, 33, 34, 35, 38, 48, 139, 141, 169	
Second Company 76, 79, 84, 88–98, 101, 122, 125	
Seifert, Anton.. 48, 59, 73, 130, 133, 134, 135, 138, 149, 150, 154, 174, 175, 176, 185, 213, 217	
Seituah	73
"Servants" of Zinzendorf.... 30, 31, 46, 51, 70, 79, 87, 89, 94, 160, 164, 165	
Seybold, Matthias 92, 103, 156, 201	
Shamokin	224
Sickness 69, 79, 83, 138, 156, 157, 158, 185, 212, 213, 214, 221, 228	
Silkhope	228
Simmonds, The 97, 98, 101	
Sitkovius 90, 91	
Skidaway Island	73
Smith House	198
"Society" .... see Gemeinschaft.	
Society for the Propagation of Christian Knowledge.. 19, 44, 50, 54	
Somers, Benjamin	217
South Carolina 14, 15, 53, 89, 226	
Spangenberg, August Gottlieb ...... 35, 36, 41–43, 45, 47, 48, 50–54, 58, 59, 60, 64, 65, 66, 68–75, 77, 78, 81–88, 94, 97, 120, 122–126, 128–131, 136, 138–142, 168–173, 177–184, 190, 199, 203, 217, 229, 230, 232.	
Spangenberg's Hymn	61
Spaniards 70, 75, 148, 161, 162, 163, 166	
Spanish War 154, 161–169, 172, 215	

INDEX. 251

	PAGE.
Spener, Philip Jacob	24, 25
Sterling's Bluff	74
St. Simon's Island	127, 128, 208, 211
St. Thomas	37, 90, 142, 206, 216, 218
Swiss Emigrants	52, 64, 65, 209, 211

T.

Tanneberger, David 92, 103, 156, 179, 184, 188
Tanneberger, John 92, 184
Thomas, Capt. 105
Thomson, Capt. 58, 59, 65, 88, 125
Thunderbolt 73
Töltschig, John ..... 48, 49, 59, 65, 66, 67, 70, 73, 78, 80, 83, 90, 120, 122, 129, 133, 134, 144, 145, 146, 149, 152, 153, 154, 158, 163, 164, 165, 167, 171–177, 188, 189, 190, 192, 196, 197, 198, 200, 201.
Töltschig, Judith 92, 102, 130, 154, 156, 158, 189, 215
Tomochichi 17, 18, 68, 74, 86, 126, 127, 131, 148, 150, 152–155, 160, 181, 185, 214
Town Lots 16, 52, 67, 68, 69, 78, 79, 179, 183, 228–234
Trades 48, 81, 84, 92, 130, 152, 155, 156, 180, 185, 217
Triebner 226
Trustees for Establishing the Colony of Georgia in America ..... 15, 16, 28, 29, 33, 34, 40, 47, 50–54, 58, 64, 78, 87, 89, 94, 95, 96, 147, 160, 163–169, 178, 181–184, 186, 187, 190, 204, 230.
Tübingen 25
Two Brothers, The 58, 59
Two Hundred Acre Tract 51, 70, 79
Tybee 88, 119, 123, 171, 189

U.

Union Galley, The 206
Unitas Fratrum 21–25, 28, 42, 48, 49, 90, 140, 146, 150, 166, 197, 199, 200, 201, 203, 218, 220, 226
Upper Creeks 149
Ulsperger, Samuel 20, 40, 41, 54

V.

Vat, Mr. 41
Verelst, Secy 54, 93
Vernon, James 34, 54, 58
Vollmar 97, 102, 139
Vorsteher 129
Voyages 56–65, 93, 97–121, 159, 170, 171, 189, 207, 216

W.

	PAGE.
Wachovia Tract	226, 228
Wagner, John George	225, 226, 228, 231
Waschke, Anna	92, 156, 180, 188
Waschke, George	48, 79, 158, 174, 176, 188
Waschke, Juliana Jäschke	174, 175, 188
Weintraube, Mrs.	92, 159
Wesley, Charles	98, 99, 101, 103, 105, 108, 110, 130, 143, 145, 147, 190, 205
Wesley, John	98, 99, 101, 108, 110, 113, 123, 124, 126, 128, 130, 131, 134, 135, 143–147, 149, 150, 157, 168, 173, 178, 185, 186, 190–196, 200, 201, 203, 205, 206, 223.
Wesley, Samuel	99
West Indies	37, 44, 45, 90, 204, 217, 218
Whitefield, George	191, 201, 202, 216, 217, 221, 222, 223, 227
Wiegner, Christopher (George)	34, 141
Wittenberg	20, 26
Woodruff, George	233
Wright, Sir James	230
Wynantz	97, 203

Y.

Yorkshire	99, 196–199, 208
Ysselstein	188, 192

Z.

Zeisberger, David, Jr.	188, 189, 211, 218, 219
Zeisberger, David, Sr.	92, 208, 217
Zeisberger, Rosina	92, 102, 217
Ziegenhagen	43, 54
Zinzendorf, Christian Ludwig von	125
Zinzendorf, Erdmuth Dorothea von	50, 135, 159
Zinzendorf, Nicholas Lewis von	22–31, 33–40, 42, 46, 51, 70, 71, 72, 78, 91, 94, 97, 135, 138, 140, 150, 154, 159, 160, 165, 181–184, 186, 190, 192, 200, 202–205, 223, 224, 227.

www.ingramcontent.com/pod-product-compliance
Lightning Source LLC
Chambersburg PA
CBHW030546080526
44585CB00012B/275